THE TAO
of
TRIBUTE MONEY

George Rapanos

B.S. (Pharmacy)
M.A. (Religious Studies)

Avensblume Press
1815 S. Saginaw Road
Midland, MI 48640

Published by Avensblume Press,
1815 South Saginaw Road,
Midland, Michigan 48640, U.S.A.

"Library of Congress Catalog Card Number:"
92-75845   9/00

ISBN number 0-9634591-1-2

Copyright © 1992
TXu 543578

Publisher's Cataloging in Publication
(Prepared by Quality Books Inc.)

Rapanos, George
    The Tao of tribute money: the truth lies beyond the paradox /
George Rapanos.
    p. cm.
    Includes bibliographical references and index.
    ISBN 0-9634591-1-2

    1. Spiritual life.   2. Metaphysics   3. Mysticism.   I. Title.
BL624.R375 1992
BL624.R36 1992b   291.4
                                        QBI92-20218

This book is dedicated to my beloved wife Susie for her love and undying devotion; whose kindness of heart, nobility of character, sense of duty and purity are exemplary. To our dearest darling children, Alex, Ruth, Laura, Angela, Jonas, and their spouses. To our grandchildren and to all children of the universe, for we are all children of God. And in memory of our family pets, Poochie, Kitty, and Puffball.

It is only with the heart that one can see clearly:
What is essential is invisible to the eye.

CONTENTS

The Tao is a delightful Paradox.

TAO

The Eternal Harmony of Opposites

Yin & Yang

The two basic forces in the cosmos, traditionally depicted in a sphere which symbolizes the great Ultimate or Absolute.

The truest sayings are paradoxical. And the way of the paradoxes is the way of Truth.

Who is to say what is real and what is not real . . .

The strangest things are true and the truest things are strange.

The very structure of a paradoxical state lies outside the human condition.

INTRODUCTION

Man builds no structure that outlives a good book!

The Tao of Tribute Money is a "source book" dealing with religious transcendence. "The Truth Lies Beyond the Paradox," the paradox is beyond the secular, and the religious, the finite and the infinite, and falls very much into Eastern and Western concepts of transcendence.

The book evolved from a religious revelation which I had in 1984, and is an anguished, forthright attempt to come to grips with the religious issues which I found hostile and unfriendly and contained in daily life. It is both a spiritual affirmation of my faith and an encouragement to those who wish to follow a path that may lead them to spiritual fulfillment.

It is not my intent to reveal a set of truths about God, as much as it is an attempt to convey through prose, poetry, quotations, parables and figures of mythological importance, images to reveal the Truth that lies beyond the paradox. The paradoxes serve to highlight the inherent limitations of our mind and mark off in some way the boundaries of the unknown territory where God dwells.

None of these strategies, taken in itself, is final; all of them taken together attempt to express the intuition of reality that touches the heart, and burns and stirs the soul. They intuit an inner coherence and unity of purpose as ways to explore the "unutterable source of existence" in which God, who is immortal and deathless, becomes present to us in a more conscious way.

I have written what I feel is crucial and important in describing the reality of Truth. The Truth is not finite, it is eternal. Much of what I have written has been written before. The truth is the same no matter under what name it is taught or who teaches it. Strip it of the personal coloring of the teacher and it is the same—Truth.

I would like to thank my friends, teachers, colleagues and those whose ideas I have absorbed in discussion or in reading. I also wish to thank those whose thoughts parallel mine in content and expression that have become so much a part of myself that I am not sure what is theirs and what is my own. I would like to express my gratitude to them and to ask them to forgive the omission of specific credit or attribution of authorship.

> Certain authors, speaking of their works, say, "My book," "My commentary," "My history," and so on. They would do better to say, "Our commentary," "Our history," etc., because there is in them usually more of other people's works than their own.
>
> Pascal

The foundation of this book was created out of the interplay between alternative thoughts and images that puzzle the mind. The enlightened mind fuses these images into something new that was once something old. Synthesizing these images into an individual vision is the basis of a Truth that lies beyond the paradox.

The writings in this book have had a mystical power over me and through God's grace, the precious pearl of His spirit is revealed. It is my wish that what lies hidden within this book will come forth in all its splendor and glory.

Has the truth been revealed by God to a particular person at a particular time and place, or is the realization of the truth and its expressions the result of a gradual process of reflection and contemplation by many individuals throughout the ages? I believe that individuals as historical persons are not so important as the truths they have discovered.

> A glass of Water containing the Truth was handed to a man. He refused to drink because the container did not please him by its outward shape.

I have always felt that it is not the messenger that is important, but the message. Not the glass, but the water. Not the letters, nor the words nor the eloquent bindings of the Holy Books that are important, but the spiritual message that lies hidden within.

When one is sick, he must take the medicine from the bottle before he can become well. Once he becomes well he can throw the bottle away. When one's soul is sick, he must intuit the spiritual message hidden within these scriptures and apply them to his life before he can become whole again.

There are also laws that are written that we are required to follow and obey for the sake of harmony. When man is transformed, he naturally follows these laws; not because of duty, but by choice. He does not need these laws to guide him, because it is within his basic nature to comply with the spirit of these laws. It is not so much what we do, as what spirit we do it in, that is important.

> Blessedness is not the reward for virtue but virtue itself.

> Spinoza

The messenger is important only when his whole life is a prayer and an example to be followed. When the messenger and the message become one, then the messenger's whole life is his message.

Mystical writings, art, poetry, and music bring heavenly powers down to earth. It is my desire that this work will give you a glimpse of the divine nature that lies hidden within you. It is a hidden treasure, a forgotten truth, that lies deep within every soul. This hidden treasure is more precious than silver, more precious than gold.

> A good book is the precious life-blood of a master spirit, embalmed and treasured to a life beyond life. But above all things, Truth beareth away the victory.

I consider this book to be a small contribution to man's search for the Hidden Treasure, "The Pearl of Great Worth," the love and peace that lies hidden deep within the soul of each and every one of us.

> The peace of God, which transcends all understanding.
>
> Philippians 4:7

The Truth Lies Beyond the Paradox

> Tell us therefore, What thinkest thou? Is it lawful to give tribute unto Caesar, or not?
>
> But Jesus perceived their wickedness, and said, Why tempt ye me, ye hypocrites?
>
> Show me the tribute money. And they brought unto him a penny.
>
> And he saith unto them, Whose is this image and superscription?
>
> They say unto him, Caesar's. Then saith he unto them, Render therefore unto Caesar the things which are Caesar's and unto God the things that are God's.
>
> When they had heard these words, they marveled, and left him, and went their way.
>
> Matthew 22:17-22

Divine law or human law? In our perceived reality one must pay tribute to both God and Caesar. But the Truth lies beyond these paradoxical statements. It is the intuition of Reality that touches the heart and burns and stirs the soul. God must come first. Then paying tribute unto Caesar will be just.

> Teacher, which is the greatest command-
> ment in the law?
> Jesus replied: "Love the Lord your God
> with all your heart and with all your soul and
> with all your mind."
> This is the first and greatest commandment.
> And the second is like unto it: "Love your
> neighbor as yourself."
> All the Law and the Prophets hang on these
> two commandments.
>
> Matthew 22:36-40

There is no other commandment greater than these because spiritually thy neighbor is thy Self. For as soon as we become aware of this, the miracle within us begins.

It matters not what you love but how you love. Only then will one be able to pay tribute to Caesar and render unto him what is due him. But if your allegiance is only to Caesar and you render unto him first, you will then have stifled the Truth that lies within and beyond, separated from the source of your existence.

Man can transcend his mind, the illusions of reality, and open up his heart to allow God's grace to shine through and disclose the reality of an eternal Truth. The eternal Truth, the sacred writings of God, are written upon the heart of man and the pages of the Book of Nature. Whatsoever is manifested on the pages of the universe is praise reflected back to the threshold of His most glorious Majesty.

One can only find God, peace, love, truth, and beauty within one's own consciousness, one's inner being. The true Self unfolds only when you strip away all of the illusions. Only the heart can transcend what reason can never resolve.

THE HIDDEN TREASURE
"The Pearl of Great Worth"

There is a hidden Treasure,
Most search for it in vain.
It comes down from heaven,
And it falls like the rain.

This treasure is not one of silver,
This treasure is not one of gold.
The source of this hidden treasure,
Lies deep within one's soul.

A treasure more precious than silver,
A treasure more precious than gold.
To find this hidden treasure,
You must look within your soul.[9]

One should not be obsessed with a passing love or with the objects of this world. One should be in love with the beloved and the beloved is God. This Avens flower is only a flower, but, in its transcendental form, the image and shadow of God

Take heed and see ye nothing do in vain,
No minute gone comes ever back again.

The Tao of Tribute Money

To my dearest darling children, grandchildren, great-grand-children and to all the children of the universe, for we are all children of God. We are one, in ultimate (God) consciousness, a consciousness that permeates the whole universe. A universe that is one unbounded ocean of consciousness in motion.

In Him we live and move and have our being...

Acts 17:28

I have lived over fifty years and have seen life as it really is, pain, misery, hunger, cruelty, hypocrisy, and suffering beyond belief; as well as the love, truth and beauty within the ultimate glory, wisdom and majesty of the creative evolutionary process.

My journey started in the finite consciousness of an authoritarian existence of conditional and transitory love, where disobedience was overcome with punishment, repentance, and submission. This Patriarchal Old Testament, master-servant type of conditional love fosters only self-hatred, sorrow, and guilt: the unfinished business that does not leave a soul in peace.

As I continued my journey, it brought me to the unfoldment of infinite consciousness, where unresolved estrangement is overcome by the unfoldment of reason, love, and atonement (at-one-ment), a maternal, New Testament, teacher-student type of unconditional love that fosters joy of Being, to a transcendental Truth that lies beyond the Paradox—beyond Good and Evil, and beyond earthly trappings.

Man is of two natures and exists in two realities and the Reality of Truth that lies beyond the Paradox transcends both of these realities. For paradoxes are the generators of infinity. The spiritual and mystical side of life.

17

The eternal core of truth is love—the first rule and ultimate purpose of life and of all things. The source of all existence. Man's anxieties arise from man's separation from this source; and his fulfillment lies in bringing him back to this source in order to fulfill the will of God—the soul of all things that are. Man must renounce his personal will, so as to fulfil the will of the Father. The purpose of all the true great religions is to bring man back to his (His) source.

A wise man lives with God in his heart. This is the way of calmness, forbearance, compassion, selflessness, and everlasting peace. For the heart of a good man is the sanctuary of the soul. The Soul is Divine, a ray that has emanated from the Spirit of God, to which we must endeavor to return.

The whole world is restless and confused. It will always be so as long as men set their ideals on the wrong objects. There will be no real happiness until men learn what they seek comes from within themselves and can be achieved through prayer and meditation. To become one with prayer and meditation is to become one with God: the mystical pure stream of consciousness that flows from the Garden of Eden.

> Why do you look without for that which is within you?
>
> Meister Eckhart

Meditation

Throughout the ages man has sought to look behind the veil that hides him from tomorrow, and through the ages certain men have seen by turning their gaze inward, in silent prayer, in silent meditation.

> For what is prayer, but the contemplation of the facts of life from the highest point of view.
>
> Ralph Waldo Emerson

The ancient knowledge of meditation is as old as creation, handed down in regular succession from teacher to student over a long period of time. For most, that knowledge has been lost.

The knowledge of meditation is a very important part—perhaps the most important part of the path for those who wish to experience the source of their existence, so they may understand what they believe. Meditation can be learned and it must be practiced. The Truth in meditation cannot be taught; it is the experience of "Being."

> Hard is the great path and few are they who travel it to the end.
>
> Mahabharata

Meditation is a spiritual discipline whose purpose is to achieve union with the supreme consciousness through the preparation of the mind for the immediate, nonconceptual awareness of Reality. One must silence the thinking mind and shift the awareness from the rational to the intuitive mode of consciousness. In that silence, God Himself becomes part of you.

Meditation is the process in the purification of the soul through solitude and relaxation. Achieving this state and vision through solitude is the task of each who seeks it.

Man must acquire an inner solitude no matter where or with whom he may be. He must learn to pierce the veil of things and comprehend God within them.

Meister Eckhart

Within the process of meditation there is an awareness of breathing, a recollection of forms and ideas, a restraining of one's thoughts, and the concentration and projection on the unity within.

> If you would glimpse the beauty we revere
> Look in your heart—its image will appear.[1]

It takes a great effort to transform your nature. This great effort in prayer and meditation is the alchemical change necessary and prepares the way for this transformation. Meditation detaches the mind and sentiments from the accidents and illusions of life and drives man to the center of his being.

> Endowed with a pure understanding, restraining the self with firmness, turning away from sound and other objects and abandoning love and hatred; dwelling in solitude, eating but little, controlling the speech, body and mind, ever engaged in meditation and concentration and cultivating freedom from passion; forsaking conceit and power, pride and lust, wrath and possessions, tranquil in heart and free from ego, he becomes worthy of becoming one with the imperishable.
>
> Bhagavad Gita 18:51-53

At last, by such meditations and prayers the breakthrough comes, slowly shifting its form. The breakthrough comes to an unfathomable realization that,

> I and the Father are one.   John 10:30

God cast unnumbered shadows on the earth,
On each one fixed his eyes, and each gave birth.
Thus we were born; the birds of every land
Are still his shadows—think, and understand.
If you had known this secret you would see
The link between yourselves and Majesty.
Do not reveal this truth, and God forfend
That you mistake for God Himself God's friend.
If you become the substance I propound,
You are not God, though in God you are drowned;
Those lost in Him are not the Deity—
This problem can be argued endlessly.

He is not, yet he is; what could this mean?
It is a state the mind has never seen.[1]

I am He whom I love and He whom I love is I.

Al-Hallaj, Sufi mystic

In this realization of oneness, all time ceases. This is why many people who have had a profound religious experience in meditation, have also had an experience of timelessness.

The aim of meditation is to exhaust all conceptualizations of the mind and detach it from the world of multiplicity. It is to prevent the mind from going astray, while the heart concentrates on God. Meditation is not to prove the existence of a transcendental mind, but to initiate the meditator into the experience of it. The whole of this experience, when transcended, is ultimate (God) consciousness.

> How can any external revelation help me unless it is verified by internal experience?
>
> Meister Eckhart

Meditation is used to put the believer in direct contact with the universe itself and bring him to the understanding that the only permanent reality to be found is not in the parts of existence but in the whole.

> After having sought Him in many places he found Him within.

Meditation is not a process of seeing, but of realizing that one IS one with the essence of the creative evolutionary process. It is a state of love in which the self is absent and the mind is no longer a focus of our experiences, ambitions, pursuits, passions, and desires. Love must be free from all earthly passions and desires. No soul can rest until it is detached from all creation.

> Man must desire to find truth, to be ready and free from passions, to follow it wherever he may find it, realizing how much his knowledge is clouded by passions.
>
> Pascal

Meditation frees the mind of external influences and desires and allow it to perceive its divine nature. Cleansing the mind permits the body to function free of stress and dys-ease.

What is experienced through meditation is the evaporation of the self (separate-self), and what remains is the world without an ego. The awareness that was previously understood to be observing the world is now realized to be one with it. Infinite pure consciousness pervades everywhere.

> I saw Eternity the other night
> Like a great ring of pure and endless light.
>
> William Blake

> I saw perfection's image, beauty's queen,
> A vision that no man has ever seen.[1]

Man is redeemed by the grace of God. The ultimate act of grace and beauty is compassion. Compassion, then, is the fruit of our spiritual journey. The breakthrough to the transcendent redemptive experience can be achieved by austerity and meditation in order to experience the Peace of God and gain His grace and wisdom. Wisdom is from God and is bestowed by an act of divine grace; not attained by scientific approach or by theological reasoning.

Wisdom and the means to attain it can only be apprehended through the actual experience of God's presence. Universal wisdom is not an intellectual understanding; it is an intuitive grasp of Truth above and beyond intellectual reasoning—a loving embrace with the universe as a whole.

When love has come the intellect has fled.[1]

The Intellect may bring the nonbeliever to the threshold of belief, but it must abandon him there.

Give up the intellect for love and see,
in one brief moment, all eternity.[1]

The intellect leads man towards the experience, but it will not give him the Reality of the experience.

The highest level of human achievement is direct contact with the Divine. This may come about through the merit of dedicated spiritual work, (a near death experience), or through Grace from above. Individual effort as well as grace are necessary for spiritual progress. God alone bestows His presence, grace, and wisdom on those who seek the Truth.

The truth is the end and the aim of all existence and the world originated so that truth may come and dwell therein.

Buddha

> If grace is given you from God above,
> Then you are wholly worthy of His love.[1]

Meditation and contemplation of the divine Being fosters a revelation of the omnipotent Self, which is one's divinity and dwells within us all. It is an "awakening" to the vision of God as He is, and how we and all things live and move and have our being in Him. The Self is indestructible, immortal, unborn, full, and limitless—the source of all happiness from whom all blessings flow.

> There is beauty in the sunlight,
> And the soft blue heavens above.
> Oh, the world is full of beauty,
> When the heart is full of love.

God's love and presence are but the revelation itself. The experience of pure grace sanctifies man through the gift and truth of His grace and this grace guides the initiate or pilgrim towards union with Himself. The highest revelation is that God is in every man.

> Higher, deeper, innermost, abides Another Life.

Bhagavad Gita

Our love was within God from the beginning and without end, a oneness of movement that existed before and beyond time. Biological time is in the realm of the finite. Spiritual time is in the realm of the infinite. One does not gain everlasting life in time, but in that which is prior to time.

> I am the Self, seated in the heart of all creatures.
> I am the beginning, the middle and the end of
> all beings.

Bhagavad Gita

> I am the Alpha and the Omega, the Beginning
> and the Ending, says the Lord, who is and who
> was and who is to come, the Almighty.

Revelation 1:8

We have been known and loved by God from before time. And this human soul is united to God by grace, as the flame of two lighted candles join and become one, and thereby are made holy forever. Grace is the indwelling experience of the soul in God. For grace has the same relationship to God as light has to the sun. Grace makes the soul God-like.

For the universal soul of God indwells in our soul, immortal and eternal. Our soul is the image of God in the depths of our Being. The virgin or purified soul equals the spirit of God. The Spirit of God is within us, existing as potential in all human form. The Spirit of Truth is the Self-acceptance of our innermost-Self.

> Do you not know that you are the temple of
> God, and that the Spirit of God dwells in you?

I Corinthians 3:16

> God is a Spirit, and those who worship Him
> must worship in spirit and truth.

John 4:24

By the process of meditation it is possible to realize the personal God, who is in union with the illusionary manifestations of the universe which He caused to exist, preserves and dissolves. Meditate upon him and transcend mental consciousness. Thus will you reach union with the ultimate (God) consciousness of the universe. When God is experienced, time and form disappear and a sense of peace evolves uniting us with the Infinite.

25

Let a man feel thy presence, Let him behold thee within and to him shall come peace, eternal peace.

No one is convinced of anything until he perceives and inwardly experiences that it is true. It is achieved by a contemplative communion, a process of meditation on the mysteries, illusions and transitory aspects of the existence and meaning of life.

You hear about fire, you see fire but until you experience fire you will never truly know of its reality.

Through meditation you unfold your own inherent divinity. This divinity rests within your heart. "I and my Father are one." "The kingdom of God is within you." "Ye are Gods, and all of you are the children of the most High." You are the hidden treasure, the pearl of great worth, a heart full of love, one in possession of the Holy Grail—the divine symbol of God's eternal grace. In the story of the Fisher King, Parsifal said,

"Uncle, what is your sorrow? Whom does one serve, in serving the Grail?" Then the Fisher King arose radiant and whole and the Grail shone with a greater light; the knights and ladies who served the Grail sang with joy and the waste land was delivered from its barrenness. Crops grew in the field, streams and lakes teemed with fish, cattle and sheep multiplied; for from Parsifal's question, which touched the source of life, all life was born anew.

Be the keeper of the Grail so it may heal the hearts of men.

There is a treasure in every person.

Sufi saying

Out of much sorrow comes knowledge and wisdom. Out of much knowledge and wisdom comes sorrow. Where there is sorrow, you are walking on holy ground. The only true contentment is to share in the joy and sorrow of others. The kingdom of heaven is a community of compassion. Those who love must share the fate of those they love.

> When sorrows come a man's true friends are found;
> In times of joy ten thousand gather round.[1]

Man realizes himself when he shows compassion and sacrifices himself for others. Giving your self up to God is the most precious offering you can make.

> A new commandment I give unto you. That ye
> love one another.
>
> John 13:34

> Greater love has no man than this, that a man
> lay down his life for his friends.
>
> John 15:13

As soon as we find each other, the miracle of us begins. The Kingdom of Heaven is never attained or discovered; it is realized; it is an awakening because it is already within you. Heaven is a spiritual dimension of life, the transcendent God whose throne is in the human heart.

> Like thoughts in my mind
> Thou ever dwelling art:
> If Thee I would find
> I look into my heart.

The heart is a mirror of His truth, wherein every divine quality is reflected. Life is a mirror which reflects only to deceive. Which after all is the more real, the one that mirrors itself, or the mirror it uses? But just as a steel mirror when coated with rust loses its power of reflection, so the inward spiritual sense, the eye of the heart, is blind to the celestial glory until the dark obstructions of the phenomenal self, with all its sensual contaminations, has been wholly cleared away.

The clearance, if it is to be done effectively, must be the work of God, though it demands a certain inward cooperation on the part of man. That cooperation is the basis of his religion; and the living experience is the basis of his religious belief. The true knowledge of God is not in the intellect, but in the experience of His presence, a presence that permeates the universe.

> The perfect man employs his mind as a mirror.
> It grasps nothing; it refuses nothing; it receives, but does not keep.
>
> Chuang tsu

The nameless is the root and source of all existence, reflecting in the soul of man like a mirror, until man becomes a co-worker with God.

The mind blocks access to a transcendent truth. We are trapped within the illusions of reality and thus do not have direct access to Reality itself.

To experience unity with the Divine, one must journey from appearances of reality to Reality itself by the path of contemplation and meditation. This process changes our comprehension of our perceived reality and elevates and unites us to a higher plain and state of consciousness. No soul can rise except by the loftiest flight of contemplation.

> If the doors of perception were cleansed, everything would appear to man as it is— Infinite.
>
> William Blake

We must seek spiritual communion with our source from this finite world of "Becoming," to the infinite world of "Being." Becoming involves the paradoxical unity of time and eternity at each and every moment in the ever-changing world. During contemplation, prayer, and meditation one becomes aware that God is the common denominator of the universe. If we do not use ordinary life as a basis for meditation, our meditation is bound to become something of an escape.

> I now prepare a robe of grace in answer to your prayer.

Prayer is man talking to God. Meditation is God talking to man. If God ever spoke to man in the past He also speaks to him today. Prayer and meditation can change the quality of the mind and soul of the one doing the praying.

What A Friend

What a friend we have in Jesus, All our sins and griefs to bear!
What a privilege to carry everything to God in pray'r.
O what peace we often forfeit, O what needless pain we bear,
All because we do not carry everything to God in pray'r.

Have we trials and temptations? Is there trouble anywhere?
We should never be discouraged, Take it to the Lord in pray'r.
Can we find a friend so faithful, Who will all our sorrows share?
Jesus knows our every weakness, Take it to the Lord in pray'r.

Are we weak and heavy-laden? Cumbered with a load of care?
Precious Savior, still our refuge, take it to the Lord in Pray'r.
Do thy friends despise, forsake Thee? Take it to the Lord in prayer;
In His arms He'll take and shield thee, Thou wilt find a solace there.[10]

> The solitude within where dwells the immortal spirit.

Prayer takes us from restlessness to solitude and tranquility to divine development, from poles of multiplicity to the one of unity.

29

The Daffodils

For oft, when on my couch I lie
In vacant or in pensive mood,
They flash upon the inward eye
Which is the bliss of solitude:
And then my heart with pleasure fills,
And dances with the daffodils.

Wordsworth

One must discover the reality of a Self-subsisting Unity in the realm of time and space.

Our origin as well as our end is Unity and nothing else. We live amidst a multiplicity which is false and unreal.

al-Jami

Your center is the very heart and core of the Universe. Out of one's center all forces are reached, all-embracing with a desire to be dissolved and absorbed, a state of existence, transcendent and divine.

God is at the center of all life! An all-embracing divine unity.

If you were at this center, you would know everything, could see all that has been and all that is to come. A man who sees the God-consciousness in everything—be it animal, vegetable or mineral—will perceive God in His presence, for this man truly sees.

Once someone asked a dervish to portray
The nature of this world in which we stray.
He said: "This various world is like a toy—
A coloured palm-tree given to a boy,
But made of wax—now knead it in your fist.
And there's the wax of which its shapes consist;

The lovely forms and colours are undone,
And what seemed many things is only one.
All things are one—there isn't any two;
It isn't me who speaks; it isn't you."[1]

When man is consciously aware of the omnipresence of God, he accepts, submits, and totally surrenders himself to this presence. All veils are lifted from the illusions of finite reality to infinite bliss. Only the individual himself can pierce the veil that hides him from tomorrow.

Knowledge will pour in upon one who stands at the center. By virtue of the mind's power man will unite all of God's attributes, wonderful gifts and abilities within himself and use them at will. He will be the perfect, wise, unsurpassable, religious man.

You cannot be born in a religion. Religion has to be born in you. You have to give birth to something from the unknown. That is the metaphorical meaning of Jesus' virgin birth. Religion is an inner revolution. It is not the temple, the mosque, or the church.

> A weak man is in <u>need</u> of religion. A religious man has no <u>need</u> for (structured) religion.

31

Sanskrit OM symbolizes
Hinduism's divine principle

Religion

Is the universe the work of God
or the symphony of nature?

In the beginning God caused the heavens and the earth to exist. All of creation was caused to exist by the thoughts and word of God.

In the beginning was the Word, and the Word was with God, and the Word was God.

John 1:1

In the Jewish religion, its scriptures, the Torah, is the Word of God, and it existed before time. In the Muslim religion, its scripture, the Quran, is the Word of God, and it existed before time. In the Christian religion, Jesus was the Word of God and he existed before time. All were revelations from God and existed before time.

We are also revelations from the Word of God and we existed before time. The Bibles and sacred writings must be destroyed together with the universe itself before a man can be free as God was until its creation.

Truth is as ancient as creation, handed down through the ages by the Masters who saw the truth of the Self. The reason for revelation is love and love existed before time. The purpose of any revelation is love. Love is the measure of His existence here on earth. In this love we have our being and in this love He serves us and we serve Him. The teachings of Christ are simply one link in the immeasurable chain of revelation, an infinitely small but indispensable portion of the great whole, which began with the world's beginning, and stretches into the Church of our own time.

All religions are really one; they are branches of the same tree, and the purpose of religion is for the welfare of all mankind, to lead him on the path of reason, devotion, love, and selfless service. The task of religion is to reach, feel, and experience the Absolute, in which all opposites are resolved and transcended into the Reality of the Truth that lies within and beyond the Paradox. Man is resurrected out of nothingness and completely transformed into an absolute Self in which the multiplicity becomes visible again, but in a changed form. In this state one acts completely through the knowledge and wisdom of God.

God and the world are one "Being," one presence in which mind and matter, creator or created, subject or object, seer or seen, knower and the known are one and the same.

> There is none beside me.   Jehovah

Barriers between opposites do not exist. They are but two ways of approaching Reality. Reality and our perception of it are one and the same. To know Reality is to be Reality. Reality is a state of "Being." The Truth lies beyond the subject-object duality, beyond good and evil, love and hate, right and wrong, pleasure and pain, night and day, life and death. Beyond free will and determinism (fate), energy and matter, particle and wave, finite and infinite. Since the two are aspects of a single reality, each is important in its own way. Evil and darkness are temporary, and the Light or God is eternal.

> Whoever reaches to his hidden sun
> Surpasses good and evil and knows the One.
> This good and evil are here while you are here;
> Surpass yourself and they will disappear.[1]

There is no subject or object, good or evil when meditation has transformed your being to a Christ- or Buddha-conscious mind. God's manifestations imply dualism in varying degrees between God and the world, and contradict the fundamental truth that "Being" is One.

> Are you perceiving the universe or are you an extension of the universe?

The relationship of God and the world's existence is one of Self-uncovering or Self-revelation. The eye in which I see God is the same eye in which God sees me. My eye and God's eye are one eye and one seeing and one knowing and one loving.

The seeker is nothing other than the inner Witness of everything which is sought. The knower and the known are one. God in one with His finite manifestations. The One sees the sun, clouds, stars, and moon, but cannot itself be seen. It hears the birds, the crickets, the singing waterfall, but cannot be heard. It grasps the fallen leaf, the crusted rock, the knotted branch, but cannot itself be grasped, because it is the very grasping itself.

> Follow it and behold, it escapes you; run from it and it follows you close. You can neither possess it nor have done with it. Henceforth, there will be no need to grieve or to worry about such things.
>
> Huang Po

> You cannot take hold of it, nor can you get rid of it; while you can do neither, it goes its own way.
>
> Yung-chia Ta-shin

Consciousness and the universe are not separate entities when the universe ceases to be objective. The perceiver is one with the universe that it perceives, so that the objective universe as well as the subjective self disappears into pure non-dual awareness.

> When I heard the temple bell ring, suddenly there was no bell and no I, just the ringing.

Thought and the object are one. Is there an observer who observes, or is there only the observing? Is there a

35

thinker who thinks the thought, or is there just the thought? Is there a knower who knows, or is there just the knowing? Is there one who hears the temple bell ringing, or just the ringing, or are the two identical? Does the drop return to the ocean, or is the ocean poured into a drop?

From this point of view, as God is beyond all dualities and pairs of opposites, the unutterable source of existence is neither finite nor infinite, identity nor non-identity, physical nor mental, duality nor nonduality, but beyond both. The Source of consciousness and the Reality of Truth lie beyond the Paradox.

I prayed that I might have a soul more than equal to, far beyond my conception of these things of the past, the present and the fullness of all life. Not only equal to these but beyond, higher and more powerful than I could imagine. That I might take from all their energy, grandeur and beauty and gather it into me. That my soul might be more than the cosmos of life.

That I might have the deepest of soul life, the deepest of all, deeper far than all this greatness of the visible universe and even of the invisible; that I might have a fullness of soul till now unknown and utterly beyond my own conception.[5]

You will know in due course that your glory lies where you cease to exist.

Ramana Maharshi

Mind is like a mirror and the dust gathers on it. Clean or remove the dust and you are Enlightened.

Shen Haiu

Seer-seen.   Knower-known.   Subject-object.   Observer-observed.

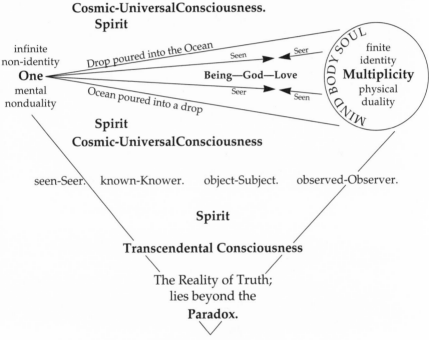

Cosmic-UniversalConsciousness.
Spirit

infinite non-identity
One
mental nonduality

Drop poured into the Ocean

Seen → ← Seer

Being—God—Love

Seer → ← Seen

Ocean poured into a drop

finite identity
Multiplicity
physical duality

MIND BODY SOUL

Spirit
Cosmic-UniversalConsciousness

seen-Seer.   known-Knower.   object-Subject.   observed-Observer.

Spirit

Transcendental Consciousness

The Reality of Truth;
lies beyond the
Paradox.

Tao. Non-Being. Void. Abyss. Annihilation. Godhead.
An Unutterable Source of Existence

The Tao that can be expressed in words is not the eternal Tao.

Lao-tse

There is no mind and there is no mirror, so where can the dust gather? One who knows this is Enlightened.

Hue Neng

All things in the world come from being. And being comes from non-being.

In relative consciousness an enlightened state is the awareness of an all-pervading unity. Opposites are no longer perceived as separate entities, but as complementary aspects in different forms of the same thing.

In absolute consciousness everything is a manifestation of that which is beyond words, beyond concept, beyond form, beyond even time and space. It is a truth that lies within, and beyond the Paradox.

> The King invited the most important people in his kingdom to a banquet to be held in his honor. When a little old man arrived dressed in rags, he was taken to the King who upon seeing him shouted, "Who are you and what do you want? You look like a beggar."
>
> The old man took this with stoical good grace and replied, "You invited me." "Not so!" cried the King, "I only invited the most important people in my kingdom."
>
> "I am important," said the old man. "Are you a mayor?" asked the King. "Much higher," replied the old man. "Are you a governor?" "Higher still," answered the old man. To this the King shouted, "Who do you think you are, God?"
>
> "Higher still," answered the old man. "There is no one higher than God," cried the King. "That's me," answered the old man.

An Unutterable Source of Existence
Infinitely Higher Than Deity

The Reality of Truth is actually neither one nor many. It is a non-dual experience within and beyond the nature of the Paradox.

There is neither creation nor destruction, neither destiny nor free-will, neither path nor achievement; This is the final truth.

Ramana Maharshi

God is immanent as well as transcendent. Just as a spider spreads out and draws in the thread that it spins, as the cloak testifies to the existence of the weaver, the door to the carpenter and the house to the builder, so too the world testifies to the existence of God.

Consider an objective creation, a silver chain. The chain did not exist before it was made, but the material, silver, was there. After the chain is made, silver still exists. If the chain is broken or melted, the chain will be gone, but silver will still remain. If silver exists before the chain was made, after the chain is broken, and while the chain is whole, then where is the chain?

Imagine that a man knows what silver is, but does not know what a chain is and wants to see one. You show him the chain, but he will call it silver. A chain consists of links, and every link is nothing but silver. Where, then, is the chain? He recognizes only silver. You have to accept that he is right; there is no reality, except silver, for the word "chain." It is only by common consent we call the object a chain. Chain is therefore only the name for a particular form.

In life man must be conscious of a dialectic nature rather than a dualistic one. That which is to be known reveals itself through the functioning of all the organs of perception, but it is free from all of them. Uninvolved, it sustains all creation; free from all experiences, it enjoys all.

God is immanent because God's existence is the existence of the world, insofar as He is one with the world. He is one with the world in being, as well as all the attributes, acts, experiences and expressions in those choosing to follow Him. He is transcended insofar as He is different from the world. He is different from the world only in attributes which He does not share with the world, such as His limitless nature, rule, and guidance.

The "unutterable source of existence," is in all, distinct from all, and greater than all. This realization transcends opposites of finite existence and unites them to become one with the absolute moment of infinite consciousness. In a finite existence, God is greater than man. In infinite consciousness, God and man are One.

Enlightenment arises when perceptions of God and the world cease to exist and the soul discerns the truth.

> A hundred thousand veils of dark and light
> Withdraw His presence from our mortal sight.
> And in both worlds no being shares the throne
> That marks God's power and His alone.[1]

Release yourself from this world and the next, and when you have turned from both, you will have perceived His hidden secrets. You will be gone and only God will exist.

> O my Lord whatever share of this world Thou dost bestow on me, bestow it on thine enemies and whatever share of the next world thou doest give me, give it to thy friends. Thou art enough for me.
>
> Rabi'a el-'Adawiyya

What is most important is not the philosophical conclusion derived from the experience, but the experience itself and the effects it has on the integrity of the life of an individual soul. One cannot experience the process of enlightenment with you, anymore than one can eat and digest your food for you. All one can do is bring the food to your table. The rest is up to you. There is no enlightenment outside of oneself.

The experience indeed reveals the true nature of reality, but this is such that human intelligence can not grasp it, nor human language express it. It is inexpressible because it is a truth that lies beyond the paradoxes of life. It is an awareness that transforms one's life.

It is a mistake to try to define our thoughts and our personal experiences of this presence that many call God in human terms. That in itself is a form of irreverence. It is like trying to put the ocean into a bottle. The god that can be expressed in words is not the eternal God.

> Can God be omniscient and omnipotent that he could create a stone large enough that even he could not lift?
>
> Riddle

Words are inadequate when attempting to express the divine nature and presence of God. The essence is too big; the essence has no limits. It cannot have, and be what it is—omnipotent, omnipresent and omniscient.

We have to do things, good for their own sake, without any hope of reward. We should not endeavor to follow our own will, but should raise ourselves to submit to whatever is the will of God. Everlasting life is to fulfil the will of God.

> Not my will but thine.
> Thy will be done.

Most religions represent different concepts. Hinduism, God as being; Buddhism, God as becoming; Taoism, becoming as the journey; Judaism, journey as history; Christianity, history as salvation; and Mysticism, salvation as surrender. The concept of Judaism represents, in part, the history of a few thousand years, but history should be perceived as evolving from the beginning of creation until the end of time.

Time is in our finite consciousness. The total process of creative evolution, the absolute history of the universe from the beginning to the end of time, is in our infinite consciousness, a consciousness that is inseparable from its parts and the rest of the universe.

God's infinite consciousness existed before time as potential energy and caused time to exist as form in finite manifested energy.

> The pure energy of things may flow together with that of our souls and both gush forth together as one stream.

Schelling

Absolute and relative existence are two complementary aspects of eternal "Being," never changing in the absolute state and forever changing in its relative state. It is like a river forever flowing, and yet one can never step into the same river twice.

The whole of creation is a manifestation of energy, the infinite reflections of One Reality, a primal energy that some call God. "Energy" is a metaphor expressing the Absolute. It is neither created nor destroyed and remains forever constant, nevertheless undergoes transformation and is manifested in various "illusionary forms." Potential energy is Absolute and the ultimate life principle of nature in various forms. It is the basis for the forces of cosmic law in the natural creative evolutionary order of the universe.

The universe evolved from a union of protons and electrons to form inorganic and organic compounds to what exists today and what will exist tomorrow. Many thousands who have died before us might claim to be joint owners with ourselves of the particles that compose our mortal bodies. We cannot say that there is a single atom of our blood or body, the ownership of which some other soul might not dispute with us. The eternal judge, the eternal spirit, constitutes the one individual soul of the universe which alone caused to exist, contained and gave life to the whole. For He alone possesses all power. He willed and the world appeared. He is the cause of the mysterious life of man into whom he has breathed a part of his own.

The Spirit of God is within you, because you are part of the cosmos, pervading all things in the creative evolutionary process of life. The human brain itself is millions of years old, and over that vast expanse of time, by its own nature and as a matter of course, evolved certain basic ways of perceiving and grasping reality. Millions of years of ancestral experience are stored up in the instinctive reactions of organic matter, and in the functions of the body there is incorporated a living knowledge, almost universal in scope, as one of primordial wisdom. Within man lives the spirit of his ancestors. The Self is here felt to be identical with the body and with the world of the ancestors, who represent the ancestral experience within us. We are all descendents of some past traveler.

The adaptation of instinct to environment is unconscious, and the wisdom of these instincts is real and comes by an illumination, a momentary uprising of consciousness like a flash of revelation, simple, historic, allegorical, and mystical. It lived before man, and will not die with him.

All religions are outer faces of an inner truth. These outer faces are the stone walls which a prison makes and the iron bars that surround a cage.

To Althea from Prison (excerpt)

Stone walls do not a prison make,
　　Nor iron bars a cage;
Minds innocent and quiet take
　　That for a hermitage:

If I have freedom in my love,
　　And in my soul am free,
Angels alone that soar above,
　　Enjoy such liberty.

Richard Lovelace

The inner truth is when one has perfect spiritual freedom in spite of the stone walls of a prison and the iron bars of a cage, as symbolized by dogmas of traditional religions which profess that God is love, rather than that God is the living experience and essence of love. It is not professing a belief, but experiencing the Truth within oneself that is essential. The kingdom of Heaven is within you. I know! I believe because I know! I'm humbled by knowing He exists.

For many, life would not be tolerable if they did not set up religious organizations and attach themselves to beliefs and ideals that are claimed for them and are presented to them, ready-made. These people cling to those unfortunate beliefs that at least provide the security of a known misery, rather than leave themselves open to a risk that is unknown or untried.

He who possesses science and art
also has religion,
but he who possesses neither of the two,
let him have religion!

Goethe

44

> The ritual of him who has seen the Truth is above anger and kindness, infidelity and religion...
>
> Mathnawi, IV

If the person believes that the ultimate is some sort of a big parent who watches after all of his children as a shepherd watches over his sheep, then that person's notion of religion is petitionary.

The aim of his religion is simply to receive protection and benediction from that God and in turn to worship and give thanks. He lives in accord with what he believes to be God's laws, and generally hopes, as a reward, to be able to live forever in some sort of heaven. The aim of this type of religion is to be saved, saved from pain, saved from suffering, saved from evil, saved ultimately from death. This type of worship is only a delusion.

> O God! if I worship Thee out of fear of Hell, burn me in Hell; and if I worship Thee in hope of Paradise, exclude me from Paradise; but if I worship Thee for Thine own sake, withhold not Thine everlasting beauty!
>
> Rabi'a el-'Adawiyya
>
> Though hell were not his fear nor heaven his goal, The Lord should wholly occupy man's soul.[1]

A religious ideal without the personal experience with the living God is a delusion. Eliminating such delusions is what reveals the face of glory, the awareness and essence of God. It is a matter of perception.

In cell and cloister, in monastery and synagogue,
Here, one fears hell, another dreams of paradise.
But he who knows the true secrets of his God
Has planted not such seeds within his heart.

Omar Khayyam

All religious doctrines are limited truths and lack verification. If any doctrines are to be the Truth, they must be experienced. The maintenance of human society is based on the majority of men believing in these doctrines for their own self-interest.

The collective mind does not progress far from animal worship to idolatry in some present day religions and beliefs. Man's helplessness and need for protection fosters the formations of many religions and religious beliefs.

This form of security lies in the projection of peace from without, and not the peace that comes from within. Enlightenment does not come through an intellectual change of opinion, but through an awakening, a religious experience followed by a rebirth to another mode of being that brings about the desired faith. The faith that is born of God overcomes the evil in the world. It is the faith experienced in the love of God's grace.

This much we know and all religions teach it: there is in everyone of us a spark of the infinite goodness out of His very nature which caused us to exist. And when we leave this earth we are reunited with it as a rain drop falling from heaven is at last reunited with the ocean which gave it birth. When grasped, this will save man from drowning in the sea of multiplicity.

She was a drop returned to Truth's great sea;
She left this world, and so like wind, must we.[1]

Our existence is a prison and this life a penance. The remedy is that we acknowledge that God is with us, protecting us and leading us into fullness and joy. Time is no longer a hindrance, but the means of making actual what is potential and lies dormant.

At the base of consciousness lies the ultimate wholeness, but the vast majority of people are not consciously aware of this truth. It is not set apart, divorced, or separated from men and women, rather it is ever present, but unrealized. It comes by way of enlightenment, an awakening to one's true nature. It is given, but rarely discovered; it is the basic nature of human beings, but lies asleep in the depths of our soul.

> Our birth is but a sleep and a forgetting,
> The soul that rises with us, our life's star,
> Hath elsewhere had its setting,
> And cometh from afar.
> Not in entire forgetfulness,
> And not in utter nakedness,
> But trailing clouds of glory do we come,
> From God, who is our home.

> Wordsworth

Creation is the theological fall of man from the Garden of Eden, marking the illusory separation of all things from the Spirit. It is our separation from God, from the "tree of eternal life." What prevents the return to the spirit is mankind's ignorance of God.

> And the Lord God commanded the man, saying, "From any tree of the garden you may eat freely;
> "But from the tree of the knowledge of good and evil you shall not eat, for in the day that you eat from it you shall surely die."

> Genesis 2:16-17

The creative Spirit thought one way, and Adam and Eve thought another, and since the thought of the creating Spirit is the origin of life, this difference of opinion, naturally, resulted in a separation.

> To set the mind on what is unspiritual is death, but to set the mind on the Spirit is life and peace.
>
> Romans 8:6

Our eating of the fruit from the tree of knowledge of good and evil symbolizes this separation as the death of the creating Spirit. Creation predisposes all levels to forget the Source, but their forgetting is what prevents their return.

The separate-self (ego) is a death from the creating Spirit. From the standpoint of the Bible, the rest of history is devoted to getting rid of the difference of opinion. The death of the separate-self (ego) is a return to the creating Spirit, "the tree of eternal life."

When man ate the fruit from the tree of knowledge of good and evil, he died to his spiritual Self. The separated self, having lost the paradise of innocence, is forever wandering in this world of woe seeking God, the soul of us all, in order to regain the peace and security he once had.

> Thou hast created us for thyself, and our heart knows no rest until it may repose in thee...
>
> Saint Augustine

A thin veil separates God from the world of matter and sense. Man must become conscious of his inborn nature that was in existence prior to creation, over which ignorance had cast its veil. Every soul passes through this veil in its journey towards birth; thus the child is born weeping, for the soul knows its separation from God. And when the child cries in its sleep, it is because the soul remembers something of what it has lost.

On parent knees, a naked new-born child,
Weeping thou sat'st while all around thee smiled.
So live, that sinking in thy last long sleep,
Calm thou may'st smile while all around thee weep.

Jalaludin Rumi

The passage through the veil has brought with it forgetfulness. He is now, as it were, in prison in his body, separated from God by this curtain. He is like the wandering stranger, separated forever, tapping on window panes because he was weaned too soon.

It is the voice of the wanderer, I heard her explain, "You have weaned me too soon, you must nurse me again." She taps as she pauses each window pane. Pray does she not know that she taps in vain. No man has seen her this pitiful ghost. And no women either has heard her as most. Sighing and tapping and sighing again. "You have weaned me too soon. You must nurse me again."

We are so created that we are strangers in the universe and our soul naturally longs for God. We are restless until we rest in Him. It is the cry of the human soul for rest, and as long as man is less than an angel and more than a beast, this cry will not for a moment fail to make itself heard.

Gods, gods! How sad the evening earth! How mysterious the mists over the bogs! Whoever has wandered in these mists, whoever suffered deeply before death, whoever flew over this earth burdened beyond human strength knows it. The weary one knows it. And he leaves without regret the mists of the earth, its swamps and rivers, and yields himself with an easy heart to the hands of death, with a premonition that it alone can bring eternal peace.

The Mater and Margarita
Mikhail Bulgakov

As a man travels through life, he has an unresolved estrangement from God, his true nature. He was weaned too soon from the realization of God, who is forever seeking him in order for him to regain the peace and security he once possessed.

He is a lonely figure standing out against "the perils of the world," with hopes of changing the course of mankind by transforming himself. Self-transformation is the true aim of the quest of the individual "against the perils of the soul."

Something absolutely new arises out of the death of the old. The true hero is one who brings the new and shatters the fabric of old values and traditions that strive to obstruct the birth of the new.

Love drives the wandering pilgrim on his quest.[1]

It is in essence the aspiration of the soul seeking to resolve this estrangement in the dark regions of the world he is wandering through, to be at peace and one with God.

Through the unfolding of reason, love, light, power and atonement, one resolves this estrangement and a synthesis occurs. This synthesis, the reunion of the soul with God, is the second birth and therein lies man's destiny—absolute freedom and immortality. May God help all those homeless wanderers.

> I tell you the truth, unless a man is born again,
> he cannot see the kingdom of God.

John 3: 3

The natural and fundamental essence of the human spirit molds the transforming process that is to be held up as a human ideal and an example to be followed. The liberating effect this has upon the world is only secondary.

The theme of the wanderer is characteristic of the stages of the soul's long journey in the process of purification. It is the alchemical transformation of the soul into the spirit. The soul is in a state of banishment. It wanders unrecognized among men. God has covered it with a veil that keeps it from being recognized by those who do not hear His voice.

> By pain and grief the pilgrim is perplexed
> But struggles on through this world and the next—
> And if the goal seems endlessly concealed,
> Do not give up your quest; refuse to yield.[1]

Resist that which resists

The separate-self (ego) lies hidden in the shadow. He is the "keeper of the gate" and the guardian of the threshold. The further inward you move, the deeper you will find the ego, which is the barrier. The way to the Self lies through him. Behind the dark aspect he represents, there stands the aspect of wholeness. Only by making friends with the shadow do we gain the friendship of the Self. Friendship towards others is rooted in the ability to be friends to oneself. Drop the barrier and you become God-like.

51

Resist that which resists. Become aware of the ego's resistance to the immediate here and now. Through spiritual practices we become aware of how the mind (ego), by having great expectations for the future and by dwelling on the past, resists the Truth that exists from moment to moment. Being conscious of its resistance, we will be able to accept it for what it is and let go of its alienating and debilitating effects. True spiritual practices expose, frustrate, undermine, and dissolve resistance to this Truth.

A certain king in India, who was of a very realistic and logical mind, went to Shankara to receive instructions as to the nature of the Absolute. When Shankara taught him to regard all of his kingly wealth and power as no more than mere phenomenal illusions arising out of the absolute Self which is the ground of all things, the king was incredulous. And when he was told that the one and only Self appeared multiple only because of the dualisms of his ignorance, the king straight-away decided to put Shankara to a test and determine if the sage really felt this existence was no different from a dream.

The following day, as Shankara was approaching the palace to deliver his next lecture to the king, a huge and heat-maddened elephant was deliberately turned loose and aimed in Shankara's direction. As soon as the sage saw the elephant charging, he turned and fled in an apparently very cowardly fashion, and as the animal nearly reached him, he disappeared from sight. When the king found him, he was perched at the top of a lofty palm tree, which he had ascended with remarkable dexterity. The elephant was caught and caged, and the famous Shankara, perspiration pouring off him, came before his student.

The king naturally apologized for such an unfortunate and nearly fatal accident. Then, with a smile breaking across his face, but pretending great seriousness, he asked why the venerable sage had resorted to physical flight, since surely he was aware that the elephant was of a purely illusory character.

Shankara replied, "Indeed, in highest truth, the elephant is non-real and illusory. Nevertheless, you and I are as non-real as that elephant. Only your ignorance, clouding the truth with this spectacle of non-real phenomenality, made your Highness see illusory me go up a non-real tree."

Self-knowledge destroys all illusions caused by self-ignorance. For until we see how we resist the path to God, your efforts to achieve it will be in vain, because what you are trying to achieve is also what you are unconsciously resisting and trying to prevent. This resistance to God's will is our real difficulty.

> For that which sees resistance is itself free of resistance.

Spiritual truth clothed in images, allegorical analogies, sacred commentaries, symbols, parables, and fables contains meaning only to those who were initiated into the mysteries that were hidden by a veil. The presence of the image is not the existence of the object. The presence of the world is like the presence of an image of an object in a mirror. The object is there before the mirror, but the image, though it appears to be behind the mirror, is an illusion.

As the presence of the image does not entitle us to say that there are two objects there, similarly the presence of the world does not justify the assertion that there is a duality of being, a world existing besides God. What imparts to it a shadow existence—a semblance of reality—and elevates it from absolute nothingness and gives it a permanence and stability is the reflection of God's existence, eternal spirit and attributes on it. It is both unreal and real, as non-real reality, a reflection of "Being" that sustains these non-beings.

The very seeing of the resistance is the dissolution of the resistance, and the acknowledgement of God's eternal presence. One must strip away the illusions of the mind before he can evolve and experience his true Self: the God within.

Let him regain his Kingdom!

Bhagavad Gita

The separation and the wandering are necessary stages in the process of purification: the purifying and transforming power of divine love.

A far, far distant land,
Is Paradise, I know.
Its presence is now at hand,
For those who want to go.

Having lost paradise, man has become the eternal wanderer. He is tormented and driven to overcome this separation by lifting the fallen soul to a state of perfection in harmony with the nurturing spirit of love, the very goal towards which all life is tending.

The hour for your departure draws near. If you will but forget all else and pay sole regard to the helmsman of your soul and the divine spark within you. If you will but exchange your fear of having to end your life someday for fear of failing even to begin it on nature's true principles, you can yet become a man, worthy of the universe that gave you birth, instead of a stranger in your homeland.

Meditations Marcus Aurelius

We are forever looking through windows towards the absolute, seeking the grandeur of our ultimate destiny.

> I saw Freedom walking alone, knocking at
> doors and asking for shelter but no one heeded
> her pleas.

One must go in exile and sever his ties of blood and soil, church and state, and his dependence on God, and become a wanderer until his solitude brings him face to face with himself. Man achieves freedom from sorrow, freedom from death, and freedom from ignorance when he ceases the need to attach or cling to anything.

> Unhappy is the land that has no heroes.
> Unhappy is the land that needs heroes.

When man has achieved this freedom, he will have ceased the idolatrous worship of church and state. Then all the efforts of his journey will not have been in vain.

> Search for the Way! The door stands open, but
> Your eyes that should perceive the door are shut!
> Once someone cried to God: "Lord, let me see
> The door between us opened unto me!"
> And Rabe'eh said, "Fool to chatter so—
> When has the door been closed, I'd like to know?"[1]

The soul's passionate longing is to be reunited with God and His creation. The soul is the image and shadow of God and existed before the creation of the Universe. He lived and moved and had his being in Him and, during its earthly manifestation, is a stranger in exile, ever longing to return to his home—longing until the time comes when he realizes that he is one with the world he is wandering through.

I wandered so aimless, life filled with sin.
I wouldn't let my dear Saviour in.
Then Jesus came like a stranger in the night.
Praise the Lord, I saw the light.

Just like a blind man I wandered along.
Worries and fears, I claimed for my own.
Then like the blind man that God gave back his sight.
Praise the Lord, I saw the light.

I was a fool to wander and stray.
Strait is the gate and narrow the way.
Now I have traded the wrong for the right.
Praise the Lord, I saw the light.

I saw the light. I saw the light.
No more darkness. No more night.
Now I'm so happy, no sorrow in sight.
Praise the Lord. I saw the light.

Hank Williams

The purpose of religion is to see the light from the darkness and escape from this prison of the senses while still in this body. The body is not to be put off, it is to be refined and made spiritual. It is like a metal that has to be refined by fire and transmuted. And the Master tells the aspirant that he has the secret of this transmutation.

"We shall throw you into the fire of Spiritual Passion," he says, "And you will emerge refined."

Man should move from passion to compassion to the Truth that lies beyond the Paradox. One cannot search for the Truth, since it is present and visible at all times. The result of searching for it makes it invisible and hidden. The breakthrough to this transcendental experience comes when one accepts, surrenders, and totally submits his will to the will of God.

56

What is puzzling to an enlightened mind is that every day many a man sees death all around him and yet lives his life as if he were immortal.

A man who lived by digging graves survived
To ripe old age. A neighbor said: "You've thrived
For years, digging away in one routine—
Tell us the strangest thing you've ever seen."
He said: "All things considered, what's most strange
Is that for seventy years without change
That dog, my self, has seen me digging graves,
Yet neither dies, nor alters, nor behaves.[1]

The struggle for immortality is not a battle, but a rite of passage. The initiate obtains immortality by being swallowed up (suffering) like Jonah in the belly of the whale, returning to the womb (God presence), gaining the secret of immortality, and being reborn spiritually from the mouth of his enemy (death). The life force has one universal principle: to be ever evolving, ever expanding, ever becoming to "that which is."

That which is born of the flesh is flesh, and that which is born of the Spirit is spirit.

John 3:6

The true meaning of religion consists in a change of heart from within, rather than conformity of the mind to external requirements. Man must change in spirit rather than have the need to change his environment (or the structure of society) before there are better people to live in it.

If you go where few have gone, you will find what few have found.

Buddha

57

Most religious institutions are based on tradition, religions made for one by others, by imitation and retained by habit.

To his surprise, the husband saw his wife cut a piece from a leg of ham and place both the cut piece and the remaining leg of ham in a pan to be cooked for dinner. He asked her why she had cut the piece off. She replied that it was because her mother did it that way.

He went to the mother and asked her if she cut a piece off a roast and then placed both pieces of meat in the pan before roasting them. She said that she did, because her mother had always done it that way before her.

He went to the old woman and asked if she also prepared meat by cutting off a piece and placing both pieces in the pan. She said that she did and explained that there was a time when her family was very poor and could not afford to buy a larger pan, so she had to cut off a piece in order to fit the roast into the pan.

How deep the ruts of tradition and conformity are. One must take responsibility for his own actions. One must find the truth for himself.

Someone handed a man a pile of manure and told him that it was gold. He was told that whenever his hunger reached the point that he was near death that he should take this gold, the pile of manure, to the bank and redeem it for money to buy food in order to save himself from starvation.

Being a trusting soul this man never questioned the validity of what he had in his possession and went about life with the belief that what he had would, in the event of a crisis, save his life.

This man always followed the dictates of others. He never questioned the actions of his society, culture, religion, parents and teachers or of those he considered his superiors. He believed that what he had in his possession would give him security. What he really had was a false sense of security.

When this man's life was coming to an end and he was in desperate need of food, he took the pile of manure that he believed was gold to the bank for salvation and was told that it was worthless!

So it came to pass that this man, not having experienced the truth—the true God—for himself, died from the lack of his (His) wisdom.

Anyone who truly knows God will not die, but have eternal life. If your faith is true and pursued with a pure heart and sincere intent, the banker will eventually proceed to cash in your perceived gold in exchange for God's grace and eternal life. This faith is truly a sublime alchemy beyond all images and multiplicities. When one's belief is independent of perceptions and inferences, he gives what he believes in a chance to work, to prove itself. This is what is meant by faith. Faith in yourself is the main objective.

Everyone must have faith that he will find and claim the Truth for himself. The Truth is not action! The Truth is not mind! The Truth is not a question of doing! The Truth is simply a question of "Being."

The only way to communicate with God is in silence. There is no need to say anything. Just bowing down in silence will do. Silence is the language for prayer.

Be still and know that I am God.

This Silence is spoken of as, "The Vision of Wisdom."

Most organized religions are institutional and are only mediators of the spirit. They lack the inner Truth. Most religions became diverted from the Truth to the needs and functions of the institution, as analogized by the story of the dove.

> Once upon a time there was a dove, representing the Truth, God, and love. People worshipped this dove as divine Truth. Some thought the dove should have a home, so a cage was built to house the dove. Others thought the cage too small, so a larger one was built. Then someone felt that the cage was not elegant enough, so instead of iron, a cage was built of brass, then one of silver, then one of gold. In time, they forgot about the true essence of the dove and it came to pass that they began worshiping the cage.

The tenacity with which religious institutions and man cling to the forms indicates that they cannot enter into Truth on a higher level of consciousness. It is a misconception for religious institutions to believe that their doctrines are the only answers to salvation and immortality. Unless these religious organizations discover new direction, they can neither develop themselves nor even hope to continue to exist.

Most religions have outlived their usefulness. They only survive as mere forms without any true spiritual life. Religions, once established, live on traditions. The church exists, simply because men dread to shatter the chalice that once contained something precious. However, the founders of every religion owed their powers originally to their direct personal communication with the divine.

Many have a lack of interest in religious institutions as mediators of the Spirit. A true religious experience can only be known by those who have experienced the presence of the dove and not the institution of the cage.

The various religions are only the changing leaves and blossoms on the stem of the eternal tree. Most religions are identical in esoteric essence. All the great religions and philosophies are but the changing garments of one eternal Truth.

God of Love in the Christian religion is worshiped in the figure of Christ. Since His "Being" is not in time, and cannot be found in space, Christ in no way can be made the property of any particular religion. The existence of Jesus as God is the Christian's inability to experience God in His non-dual existence.

Jesus Christ became a messenger from God to us. Jesus to Christ is a symbol of transformation. Transformation is a kind of resurrection from the dead. Those fortunate to hear the call are being transformed into the Selfsame image. For just as Jesus Christ, we bear both humanity and divinity in us, and since we too are united in God, we share with Christ his divine origin in God.

> You will change them and they will be changed;
> but you are always the Selfsame.

> Psalms 102:26-27

> The kingdom of God is within you.

> Luke 17:21

The word was made flesh and dwelt among us and we saw His glory, glory of the Only-Begotten of the Father, full of grace and truth.

> He gave them the power to become sons of God.

> John 1:12

We see the glory of the Only-Begotten, coming from the Father through a transformation. If I fulfill the will of the Father.....

> I am in the Father and the Father is in me.

> John 14:11

I and the Father are one.

John 10:30

This is said of each of us as the son of man becomes a son of God through grace, acknowledging the Spirit as my Father. Every man in spirit is the son of God. True faith is founded on this sonship to God. Not by flesh, but by the Spirit. For He is not the God of the dead, but the God of the living. In God all are living. All men who come to know they are sons of God receive true life, doing good out of love for mankind. The only real life is the life of the son of man according to the will of God, the Father.

All the things that the Father has are mine.

John 16:15

All things that are mine are yours and yours are mine.

John 17:10

Christianity is not the only way. Salvation is not upon all who would embrace and identify with the historical Jesus. To place Christ only in history is to place him in the past, and the past is thoroughly dead, and the future is yet to be. "Christ" never was, nor will he be. "Christ" IS and lives in the consciousness of the present moment. Eternal. For before Abraham was, "I AM."

> And God said unto Moses, "I AM THAT I AM:" and he said, "Thus shalt thou say unto the children of Israel, 'I AM hath sent me unto you.'"

Exodus 3:14

If Jesus could realize his identity with God, you can, too. And to identify Jesus as the one and only historical incarnation of a divinity is only to reinforce the presumptuousness of Christianity, with all the self-righteousness of its missionary zeal. What arrogance of the person of any religion to think that theirs is the only path that leads to God.

> Your arrogance deceives you, and you stray
> Further and further from the spirits' Way.
> Your self has trapped your soul and made it blind;
> The devil's throne is your complacent mind.[1]

> A difference of opinion is what makes horse racing and missionaries.
>
> Will Rogers

Christianity believes that there is but one incarnation and that was Jesus Christ and so we cannot become incarnate.

> Of what use Gabriel, your message to Marie,
> Unless you can give the same message to me.
> That the Christ spirit should live in me,
> And through my life as well.

In Buddhism we are all incarnations of Buddha consciousness. The only thing that is required is that we should come to the knowledge of that and live out of that knowledge. Our task is to incarnate the God within.

Truth is a Divine Attribute, and the foundation of every virtue. The truth is in the Spirit, not in the word. We need, like Moses, a firsthand, immediate, and intimate experience of God. God's image and divine revelation can bestow a new spirit into the heart of man, not just a belief that somebody at sometime had an experience. All that is irrelevant unless we recognize the way in which Moses, Jesus, Buddha, Krishna, Mohammed and others give us an insight into the way in which their experiences came about that may enable us to achieve the same experience.

Jesus personified the experience because his whole life was a prayer and an example to be followed. The example of a great individual is useful to lead us on the way, for nothing is more conducive to spiritual enlightment than the power of a great example.

> No man was ever great without some portion
> of divine inspiration.
>
> Cicero

The path of Jesus is the path of love and compassion. In compassion we and our works become divine and God becomes a human once again. Jesus demonstrated how one must live in order to feel "deified." He was the "bringer of glad tidings." Jesus Christ lived this unity of God and man as his "glad tidings." This is what I believe Jesus meant when he said,

> I am the way and the truth and the life; no one
> comes to the Father, but through Me.
>
> John 14:6

Jesus reveals the way to the Father, not the Father himself. Jesus' is the way, the truth, and the life. He who believes in Jesus' simple and sublime teachings shall receive the true life. He shall receive the life of the spirit, a true way of life instead of the false way of the personal life that most men follow. This is the true life which Jesus Christ came to teach.

It is the Humanity of Jesus, far more than the Divinity of Christ, that makes the mass of Christians worship Him, far more than they do the Father. Jesus like all souls, was of the same substance with God, a manifestation of his (His) Divinity.

The mystery of life is not something which can be solved or which is ever solved. It has to be lived. True life commences only when the soul, a ray of Divine origin, is emancipated for its return and rises unimpeded to the noble source and grandeur from which it came.

> I am the light of the world; he that follows me
> shall not walk in darkness, but shall have the
> light of life.
>
> John 8:12

Jesus is the expression of a wisdom, which was also, if differently, realized in Buddha, Krishna, Chuang-tse, Lao-tse, Muhammad, Moses and many others. Denying this reality and Truth is rather like the tail denying the existence of the dog.

Love is the World's Greatest Religion

Put your hand in the hand of the man who stilled the water.
Put your hand in the hand of the man who calmed the sea.
Take a look at yourself and you may look at others differently,
By putting you hand in the hand of the man from Galilee.

*Crown of thorns and three nails
mean Christ's Passion on Cross*

Declarations of Truth

We are all story tellers and our lives are fictions that we have made. The thinnest veil separates dreams from reality.

Is truth a dream or are dreams truth?

A man had a dream that he was a butterfly. In that moment, in that reality, he was a butterfly going from flower to flower. When he awoke, he realized that he was a man having had a dream that he was a butterfly. Down deep within his thoughts, he now wonders if he really is a butterfly having a dream that he is a man.

Was it a dream or was it true?
Was I drunk or sober? I wish I knew.[1]

Why am I me, and why not you? Why am I here and why not there? When did time begin, and where does space end? Isn't life under the sun just a dream?

Could it be that our perceived reality is nothing but a declaration of reality and not Reality itself? No one can be sure whether he is awake or asleep, since during sleep we believe that we are awake as firmly as we do when we are awake.

Now our whole life from birth unto death, with all its dreams, is it not in its turn also a dream, which we take as the real life, the reality of which we do not doubt only because we do not know of the other real life? Our life is but one of the dreams of a more real life and so it is endlessly, until the very last one, the very real life—the life of God.

Letters Leo Tolstoi

The world is a dream and death of the separate-self is the morning light. The greatest of all miracles is birth.

The greatest of all mysteries is a new spiritual life out of suffering, (symbolically dying to the ego, and again entering the world regenerated, like a spotless infant). And the greatest of all adventures is the death of the mortal body.

> Prospero: You do look, my son, in a moved sort,
> As if you were dismay'd: be cheerful sir:
> Our revels now are ended: these our actors,
> As I foretold you, were all spirits, and
> Are melted into air, into thin air:
> And, like the baseless fabric of this vision
> The cloud-capp'd towers, the gorgeous palaces,
> The solemn temples, the great globe itself,
> Yea, all which it inherits, shall dissolve,
> And, like this insubstantial pageant faded,
> Leave not a rack behind: We are such stuff
> As dreams are made of, and our little life
> Is rounded with a sleep.—Sir, I am vex'd;
> Bear with my weakness; my old brain is troubled,
> Be not disturb'd with my infirmity;
> If you be pleased, retire into my cell,
> And there repose; a turn or two I'll walk,
> To still my beating mind.[4]

The ego-self cannot know God. We must experience Him through our Soul, for the soul is a spiritual traveler to be awakened to its true destiny.

Religious institutions, sacred traditions and writings, rituals, and symbols are for the human spirit windows to look through in seeking the ultimate. The mystery of rebirth is the sole object of the initiation rites. In this birth, you will discover all blessings.

The meaning of all rituals is for the purely personal to be transcended into a personal revelation of God. Symbols that appear in rituals are creative expressions of the spirit that permeate and stir the soul as visible manifestations of God.

Myth, art, religion, and language are all symbolic expressions of the creative spirit in man that liberates in us a mightier voice than our own, bringing emotional freedom and atonement by sanctifying man's personal fate with that which transcends him.

If man has not understood that the purpose of these declarations of truths is to reach God, and he simply engages in them out of duty, then he is wasting time in such engagements. The inner attitudes of reverence and devotion are more desirable than external objects and ceremonies. To some, doctrines and rituals become a bridge; to others, they become a barrier.

Do not become attached to doctrines and rituals and become confused. Persons in God-consciousness are sanctified by the Holy Spirit and transcend religious institutions, doctrines, sacred traditions and writings, rituals, and symbols. They are one with God and in communion with Truth itself. Declarations of truth are vehicles for that transforming experience. They contemplate the mysteries, illusions and transitory aspects of the existence and meaning of life.

All religions have their various beliefs. The differences are in their declaration, not in the Truth itself. A synthesis of ultimate truth underlies all such differences. Belief is not an adequate substitute for inner experience.

> Just as a candle cannot burn without fire, men
> cannot live without a spiritual life.

Buddha

Dogmas, creeds, sacred scriptures and writings are like bottles of medicines for those whose souls are spiritually sick and need help. The medicine comes in bottles of various shapes and sizes but the medicine is always the same. Once the patient is cured, he does not need the bottle any longer and is free to discard it at any time. Medicine cures the ills of the body, and Divine Truths heal the disease (dys-ease) of the soul.

> Ye preach the scriptures, because ye think that
> in them ye have eternal life.

To maintain that a particular dogma is a divine revelation inspired by the Holy Spirit is in the highest degree presumption and folly. The highest presumption, because there is nothing more arrogant than for a man to say, "What I tell you, God Himself says through my mouth."

It is necessary to take away or see beyond the external objects in which one has falsely placed his trust. The scriptures are not the doctrine of how we may make ourselves happy, but how we may make ourselves worthy of happiness.

If one surrenders his freedom to the institution and dogmas of the church, synagogue, or mosque, he does so at his own peril. There is an enormous gap between representations of God by the preachers and the actual experience itself. If religion and its religious metaphors prove archaic and stand in the way of the experience, they should be thrown out. But the ideal towards which they point must be pursued with a pure mind and sincere heart.

> Master Ganto said to his brother: "Whatever
> the great masters of Zen say, however they
> expound the Scripture, of what use is all their
> learning and understanding to another person?
> That which gushes out from your own heart—
> that is what embraces heaven and earth!"

To actualize this experience one must lay down the banner of pride, cast away the club of resentment, enter on the path and live to seek God with true faith and devotion. A service performed for the love of God.

This devotion—this surrender of one's personal identity to the will of God—will find fulfillment in the identity of the beloved. And there is gained the absolute freedom and fulfillment of life. To succeed is the greatest of all endeavors.

> The greatest conqueror is the Conqueror of self.

All religious doctrines are merely declarations of truths, but not Truth itself. God has revealed Himself and His will in the words of these holy books, which are basically one of the means by which man can know Him. These books are the scriptures of the world's religions. A wealth of knowledge is revealed within these great books of the past, and from these truths come a wellspring of experiences.

One must not confine himself to the mere knowledge and history of the saints (those great prophets and teachers of the past) but give actuality to the past through the application of this knowledge. Names are not considered to be important. How this knowledge is obtained is the only thing that is relevant.

Through words and deeds an enlightened man moves heaven and earth. Man may count on mere words to awaken faith; but to unfold to the glory that lies within, one must apply these words to deeds. We have to identify with these saints and prophets, not imitate them.

> Baso used to sit cross-legged from morning till night in constant meditation. His master saw him and asked: "Why are you sitting cross-legged in meditation?" "I am trying to become a Buddha," he answered.
>
> The master picked up a brick and began polishing it on a stone nearby. "What are you doing, Master?" asked Baso. "I am trying to turn this brick into a

mirror," was the answer. "No amount of polishing will turn the brick into a mirror, sir."

"If so, no amount of sitting cross-legged will make you into a Buddha," retorted the master.

It is not what deeds were performed by the saints and sages of the past that is important, but what disciplines were adhered to; what paths were followed; what inner experiences took place that transformed these unique individuals so that we can also benefit by the knowledge and wisdom of their journey. All religious doctrines are merely a journey towards the experience.

> The ignorant, it's true, can never share
> The secrets of our king. If one should dare
> To ape the ways of the initiate,
> What does he do but blindly imitate?[1]

Only through love can we know that we are at one with God. We must love, not in words, but by deeds, in truth. And he who so loves has a quiet heart, because he is at one with God.

Writings cannot express words completely. Words cannot express thoughts completely. Many are unable to appreciate, see, comprehend, or experience the intent of the message and what these saints, prophets, sages, and great teachers of the past related by way of these books of antiquity. Attention is called to the fact that an innate capacity is essential to an understanding of these great books.

> How blessed is the man who finds wisdom,
> And the man who gains understanding.

Proverbs 3:13

Wise men taught by way of haiku, parables, analogies, allegories, legendary myths, wisdom tails, koans, and fables, intended as vehicles of truth in order to set up images and ideas that expressed their thoughts completely.

> Those who are worthy reach
> A subtle understanding none can teach.[1]

Speech and writings are imperfect transmitters of thought or of experiences, but by means of the images and the stimuli contained in them, a spiritual force is set in motion whose action transcends the limits of time and space.

It is only through the living personality that the words of those great books ever fully come to life. The wisdom in the words of those who prophesied in these great books are not of any private interpretation. The wisdom that these books contain came by the will of spiritual and holy men. They spoke and wrote as they were moved and instructed inwardly by the Holy Spirit and outwardly by the Grace of God, which exerted God's influence upon the world to take its course according to eternal laws.

During times of rest, experience and wisdom are obtained by meditating and reflecting on the mystical and spiritual contents of these books. Infinite wisdom comes to those who are inwardly receptive. The more that one draws from this inner wealth, which is inexhaustible, the greater his experience becomes. This is the concept of the elect, the supernatural among the chosen throughout the ages.

> For each is that which he has earned and against
> each is only that which he has deserved.

Quran

Knowledge is a refreshing and vitalizing force, but one must experience these eternal truths in order to gain the wisdom from the knowledge of this history.

There came a woman of Samaria to draw water; Jesus said to her, "Give Me a drink."

For His disciples had gone away into the city to buy food.

The Samaritan woman therefore said to Him, "How is it that You, being a Jew, ask me for a drink since I am a Samaritan woman?" (For Jews have no dealings with Samaritans.)

Jesus answered and said to her, "If you knew the gift of God, and who it is who says to you, 'Give Me a drink,' you would have asked Him and He would have given you living water." (direction)

She said to Him, "Sir, You have nothing to draw with and the well is deep; where then do You get that living water?

"You are not greater than our father Jacob, are You, who gave us the well, and drank of it himself, and his sons, and his cattle?"

Jesus answered and said to her, "Everyone who drinks of this water shall thirst again; but whoever drinks of the water that I shall give him shall never thirst; but the water that I shall give him shall become in him a well of water springing up to eternal life."

John 4:7-14

The foundations of human nature are the same in everyone. Every human being can draw in the course of his education from the inexhaustible wellspring of the divine in man's nature.

A well that is fed by a spring of living water is a good well. Such a spring never runs dry. A well of water springing up into him is everlasting life.

> The tree of life is like a river of water, clear as
> crystal, coming from the throne of God.

One must drink from the spring of their words and translate them into the experience of life in order to enjoy their fullness and inexhaustible abundance, thus gaining true faith in the experience.

The all-inclusive principle of union is expressed in the spontaneous affection of love, the rapture of being alive. A life-giving activity, to which all beings owe their existence, is something purely spontaneous.

It is not like the conscious anxiety of man who strives for the good with inward toil. True joy must spring from within. Thus, the life of man who has purified and perfected himself is a light unto himself, as well as a light unto others.

> Be a light unto yourself.   Jesus
> Be a light unto others.   Buddha

One's life must be for the good of mankind in the service of humanity, and thus live life eternal.

> Let your light shine before men in such a way
> that they may see your good works and glorify
> your Father who is in heaven.

> Matthew 5:16

Pure Spirit. Those that are saved shall walk by its light, for the glory of God has illumined them. The glory of God is man deified. There shall no longer be any night and they shall not have any need of the light of a lamp, nor the light of the sun, because the Lord God shall illuminate them and they shall reign for ever and ever.

I said to the man who stood at the gate of the year; "Give me a light that I may tread safely into the unknown." And he replied, "Go out into the darkness and put thine hand into the hand of God. That shall be to thee better than light and safer than a known way."

M. Louise Haskins

Human reason without the light of God makes a light of its own. It is a light into darkness and forever separated from the glory of God's inner light.

> (Don't grieve because the Way is dark as night,
> Or strive to emulate the Sun's pure light);
> Whilst you are locked within yourself your cares
> Are worthless as your worthless cries and prayers.
> If you would soar beyond the circling sky,
> First free yourself from thoughts of "me" and "I";
> If any thought of selfhood stains your mind
> An empty void is all the self will find,
> If any taste of selfhood stays with you
> Then you are damned whatever you may do.[1]

Cast your care upon the Lord and he will support you.

Psalm 55:22

True joy, therefore, rests on firmness and strength within, revealing itself outwardly in yielding and gentle behavior. It desires nothing from without, being content within and one with everything, remaining free of all egotistical likes and dislikes.

> It's not doing the things we like to do, but liking the things we have to do, that makes life blessed.

Goethe

If we would not choose the fate or our being in the world, we can nevertheless accept and assume responsibility for our attitude towards that fate.

When man has transcended the finite conscious state of mind to be one in God-consciousness, he no longer is caught up in the struggle and turmoil of individual beings. Through acceptance, surrender and total submission to the will of God from moment to moment, man experiences a true peace of mind which is necessary to understand the wisdom of the great laws of the universe and for acting in harmony with them, thus giving hope to all mankind.

> God is a light shining itself in silent stillness.

Those who lack inner stability and therefore need amusement will always find opportunity for indulgence. They desire and attract external pleasures of the senses by the emptiness of their natures. When a person lacks peace and does not feel content with his situation, he may attempt to improve it through conflict. Passion and desire cause suffering, and corrupt from within.

> He was brave! He was strong! But he never learned how to look into men's hearts, least of all his own.

> Desire is the root of all suffering.   Buddhism

> Desire has burnt my life in its consuming fire.[1]

> Who is a strong man? He who conquers his Passions.
>
> Talmud

A man who is himself free from passion and all selfish ulterior considerations and motives, who perseveres in right, honor, justice, and truth is capable of so dissolving the hardness of egotism.

Nothing can cure the soul but the senses, just as
nothing can cure the senses but the soul. That
is one of the great secrets of life.

One develops slowly according to the law of one's
being. The development must be allowed to take its
proper course.

Dislodging a green nut from a shell is almost
impossible, but let it dry and the lightest tap
will do it.

Ramakrishna

Our soul is united to God by our goodness and is
lovingly led and strongly drawn to His revelation of
love. A simple sacrifice of selfless service offered with
real piety holds a greater blessing than an impressive
word or a service without warmth. Therefore, here on
earth, God's work must surely be our own.

The earth is man's extended body, to be loved
and respected as one's own body.

Water, in Chinese sign,
is a life-giving source

Symbols

A room or house often symbolizes the psychological framework out of which we are living. It is our psychic home in which we dwell.

Truth has been hidden under symbols, and often under a succession of allegories, where veil after veil had to be penetrated before the true light is reached, and the divine mystery of truth revealed.

Symbols and images move and awaken the mind to an infinite source of consciousness beyond their finite conscious existence. To experience personal salvation one must transcend these religious symbols and institutions with their various traditions, dogmas, doctrines, and beliefs (these spiritual personalities or messengers of divinity) in order to gain the essence and wisdom of their message and the divinities they represent.

To gain the experience and the spiritual significance of the message is more important than the messengers or the symbols that point to God's existence. These cryptic messages are from the wisdom of the soul.

Easter is represented by symbols of transformation, the sacrifice, the crucifixion, and the actual transcendence of the separate-self. "Christ has risen!" All are carried out in a self-sacrificial frame. You die as you are, and are resurrected totally new.

The sacraments are esoteric meanings of their symbols. Symbols do not render the experience, they suggest it. Christ is sacrificed (the Lamb); he dies to his separate-self (Crucifixion), and is reborn to ascend into Heaven (actual transformation). One dies to his present limited, finite, mortal self-sense, and moves from matter to spirit, from passion to compassion to the Truth that lies beyond the Paradox. Beyond Good and Evil, beyond the trappings of the world that hold man captive.

The intricately interrelated threading of the spider's web to depict the world is a profound "symbol" when understood, because the threads of the web were drawn out from within the spider's very being. Just as a spider spreads out and draws in the thread that it spins, so does God gather all that He has created. God is the center of our universe and we are never lost, if we realize the center. We are the manifestation of the Creator and, therefore, everything is sacred.

The exoteric forms of religion are the substitute forms of the absolute where God is primarily loved. What is interesting is that the obsession for worldly gratifications such as work, money, power, success, fame, and sex, as justification for existence, are also substitute forms of God. One becomes a slave if these substitute gods occupy and consume every hour of the day. They will ultimately take possession of the individual soul and its salvation and destroy him.

> For the love of money is a root of all sorts of evil, and some by longing for it have wandered away from the faith, and pierced themselves with many a pang.
>
> 1 Timothy 6:10

These legal narcotics human beings use to forget the pain of their existence are a substitute for the living experience of God as "Being." Without their false gods the alternative is natural desperation. These illusions and deceptions are necessary if one is to surrender his freedom to a false god in order to tolerate one's self and his life.

> An insomniac went to a devout doctor for advice. "Memorize prayers, and sit up all night repeating them," said the holy physician. "And will that cure my sleeplessness?" "No, but it will cease to annoy you."

Blindly and mechanically, we pursue various activities that we are conditioned to believe will bring us freedom and peace. We maintain the illusion that there is an object that could satisfy our desire so that we can engage in various activities—diversionary mechanisms to avoid self-reflection. True peace exists only through an awareness of a lack that these activities fill.

Most people's disappointments in this materialistic world stem from wanting something desperately and not being able to have it, but the greatest disappointment is wanting something desperately, getting it, and then finding that it does not fulfill one's expectations. The first holds an element of blind hope; the second an element of despair.

People literally drive themselves into blind oblivion with social games, psychological tricks—personal preoccupations so far removed from reality that they are forms of madness.

> When life itself seems lunatic who knows where madness lies. Perhaps to be practical, this is madness. To seek dreams when there is only trash, this could be madness. Too much sanity could be madness. But maddest of all is to see life as it really is and not as it should be.
>
> Man of LaMancha
> Miguel de Cervantes

The Eternal Quest

There are many roads that lead to God. Attaining His vision is the task of each one who seeks it. One path is through meditation, the preparation of the mind for immediate non-conceptual awareness of Reality, resulting in sudden enlightenment or grace. Another is through action as in song and dance, when you are unable to separate the dance from the dancer, the subject from the object, and you become one with the moment, and that moment is one in God. Another is through devotion and selfless service, and there is one that leads through the intellect.

Knowledge, devotion, action and selfless service are the only real entrances to the life of contemplation. All are interdependent and must be practiced together. The basic aim of these processes is to shift the awareness from the rational to the intuitive mode of consciousness. You will find in the end that all of these paths are but one path. Those who have become enlightened have all walked the same path, the road to enlightenment and salvation.

One's own efforts are needed if he is to satisfy his hunger and need for God. Each path varies with each individual. You would not expect the ant to travel the same path as the elephant.

> How could a spider or a tiny ant
> Tread the same path as some huge elephant?[1]

Once we experience divinity within ourselves we naturally see it in the world around us and our life becomes transformed. We hear the song of the universe and the music of the spheres. The cosmic experience is the music we dance to, not unlike being unable to separate the dance from the dancer.

There are none who cannot attain this divinity. Man must begin the eternal Quest for the meaning of existence. The goal of the quest is transformation—subsistence through God and unity of Being.

Look within....the secret is inside you.

Hui-Nen

You cannot find yourself as long as you are searching outside of yourself. This is the great secret. What is sought is the very nature of the seeker. Virtue is not something to be gained, for it is already contained in oneself. The problem of knowing the Self is illustrated by the story of the lost tenth man.

Once ten men travelling together came to a river that could only be crossed by swimming. They plunged into it and reached the other bank. Now the leader assembled the group in order to ascertain if all had reached safely and counted them. He saw only nine men. He counted again but every time, he saw only nine men. The men searched for the missing man frantically up and down the river bank, but their efforts were of no avail. The tenth man was lost. They were all filled with despair as they sat there weeping.

A Master happened to come by and inquired why they were sorrowful. The leader told him about the lost man. The Master closely scrutinized the group and smiled; he instantly understood the problem. "Don't worry," he said, "the tenth man is here; I can produce him right now." The Master asked all the men to stand in a line. No one knew how he could produce the tenth man by this exercise, but they obeyed because they had faith; not blind faith bordering on superstition, but faith pending confirmation. There was, after all, no reason to disbelieve the Master.

The Master then asked the leader to step out of the line and count the others. He began to count "One, two..." and so on up to nine. Pointing to the leader, the Master said, "You are the tenth man; you have forgotten to count yourself." The leader immediately understood; he "gained" the missing man by "realizing" that he had been the tenth man all along.

The leader (seeker) discovered that he was also the sought. As long as he was searching for the missing tenth man, he continued to miss him; it could not have occurred to him that he himself might be the tenth man, because he had already concluded that the tenth man was lost and had to be searched for.

Everyone's journey, quest, should be towards his perfection. The soul is alienated in the course of time and space, and the quest is for its reunification. God's divine grace will then guide him in this world of limited reality towards union with Himself.

Those who are attached to the phenomenal world will give excuses for not making the effort needed for the journey. When one's faculties are awakened to the inner dimension or aspect of things, he will see beyond the material world recognize his essential affinity with God, and begin the quest.

The awakened soul guided by God's celestial grace and not by nature will choose to make the journey towards complete fulfillment. At the end of the quest the enlightened person will become aware that what he sought was none other than himself. The beings of creation and the Creator are indivisible and the essence of God has always been with him, guiding him from within throughout his entire journey through life.

Initiation

If you are summoned by a distant call,
Pursue the fading sound until you fall;
And as you fall the news you longed to find
Will break at last on your bewildered mind.[1]

The object of initiation is to be sanctified. Intuition lights up the soul with rays from the Divinity, the eye with which it contemplates the field of Truth.

One must be wounded before one seeks and follows the path to enlightenment. The depth and intensity that seizes the individual is the initiation that summons the individual to begin the quest. If one wishes to take up the option of initiation, it can be the door into the inner and upper kingdoms.

Initiation is considered to be a mystical death and resurrection to life. Imperfections are purged away and placed under Divine Protection. Initiation appears spontaneously, flashing as it were, into the soul, making the soul the involuntary instrument of its utterance to the world. It's love springs up in the soul, as water gushes upward in a spring. Initiation elevates the soul, from a material, sensual, and purely human life, to a communion with God.

In receiving the eternal gift of love one becomes aware of the Self, about which the ego revolves in a perpetual paradox: identity and non-identity, reality and non-reality. Everything evolving from everything and again entering into everything. Depending on everything and connecting with everything. Releasing in us a primordial fire of direct revelation, the formless perfection of a "Supreme God." A deeper lying reality that transforms the individual and endows life with a meaning.

Thus the individual, like the ego, stands between two worlds that threaten to overwhelm him. Only the individual can stand his ground against these overwhelming collective-social forces, because he is the exemplar of individuality and possesses the light of a higher consciousness.

Each of us should be on the path seeking spiritual perfection, striving to reach the center and not the periphery. What changes in our lives is not a union with God, but a process of awakening and realizing our oneness in God from the beginning to the end.

The purpose of the initiation process is to restore to the soul the divinity it lost at birth. From this seed, if one follows the path, his spirit will grow and blossom. Only then will he realize the fruits of his labor.

> Indeed, until this glance discovers you
> Your life's a mystery without a clue.[1]

The initiation of one's return to his spiritual center is realized the moment he recognizes this separation from the core of his true Self. For at the moment, the awareness of something that we have always known is the initiation, a most profound experience and our first tentative move towards life, freedom and immortality. An unfolding to what we have always been and always will be—an intricate part of ultimate (God) consciousness within the cosmic cycle of life.

> In initiation, one "dies" to be "reborn" again.

Initiation is accompanied by the death of the individual ego (separate-self), and the rebirth of the Self (universal spirit). It connects the seeker spiritually to the infinite presence of God.

> Merging of itself with God, the Ego passes
> away.

God's spiritual presence begins with revelation. Initiation is a means of opening the door. Going in depends upon one's will.

From Separate-self to Self

If Thou hast ears to hear, receive my message clear;
With Him to link thy heart, thou must from self depart.

Not until man becomes aware of his separate-self and the devastating effect that the ego has upon the unfoldment of his true Self, will he forsake his ego and begin the quest to attain the knowledge and wisdom that lies dormant within and beyond.

The goal of the quest is the Self. The supreme attainment which is beyond mind, beyond ego, is only possible when existence itself as man knows it has been transcended, otherwise he will forever remain unenlightened.

Only when man is one with the essence of existence will a different love flower.

> Awhile, as wont may be,
> self I did claim:
> True Self I did not see,
> But heard its name.
>
> I, being self-confined,
> Self did not merit,
> Till, leaving self behind,
> Did Self inherit.

This Self-knowledge, the deity within you, is both purifying and creative. This inner purification will give you peace and strength. Peace and security are the essence of divine love. This timeless and selfless essence of immortality overshadows the physical death of the body. To enter freedom is not to die one's physical death, but to resist the ego's alienating and debilitating effect and thereby live a new Life—to live the life of the true Self.

Tender only to one, tender and true.
The petals swing to my fingering,
Is it you or you?

Tender only to one, I do not know his name.
And friends who fall to the petal's call
May think my love to blame.

Tender only to one, this petal holds a clue.
The face it shows but to those who'll know
That I am tender, too.

Tender only to one, last petals latest breath.
Cries out aloud from his icy shroud.
His name! His name! Is Death.

The spiritual "resurrection" is not of the so-called dead, but of the living who are dead in the sense of not having entered upon true life. To overcome death, one only has to die to the separate-self and then this union of Self with God can know no death.

> Truly, truly, I say unto you, unless a grain of wheat falls into the earth and dies, (the separate-self, the ego) it remains alone; but if it dies, it bears much fruit.
>
> John 12:24

When the separate-self sense dies, all that dies is only the illusion the mind (ego) has created. When the ego is in control in the realm of time and space, your heart is a captive and your soul is afraid. Once the ego has created the illusion, it clings to life out of the fear of its own death. Our fear is purely an abstract concept based on the illusion that each of us will live forever.

> Life must be considered as a loan that carries a greater obligation than if it were a gift.

Once the separate-self is united with its source of existence, it transcends death, and the soul is released from the strictures of time and space.

> God makes you die to yourself and live by Him.
>
> Junayd

Shakespeare said that a city is made up of strange streets and death is the marketplace. It also can be said that religions are like unto strange streets, and God is the marketplace. All roads lead to God.

> The ocean is the goal of all streams and of the rain from the clouds.

The very final stage of the journey is the return to the market-place, where your true Self had never left. You were there all the time. It is a return to wholeness—our divine origin. And this return is what salvation is about.

> At the end of the quest we will arrive where we started and know the place for the first time.

If one relates to his death with fear, then for him the Spirit (God) is dead. If one transcends the ego the mind has created, he will experience a union of Self with the source of his (His) existence. This union overcomes the fear of death and he is now one with the Spirit of God in the marketplace. Man should not be afraid to die any more than he was to be born.

The mind devoid of all fear, free from all forms of attachment is master of itself. It then follows its own course like water down a stream.

From too much love of living,
     From hope and fear set free,
We thank with brief thanksgiving
     Whatever gods may be
That no life lives forever;
That dead men rise up never;
That even the weariest river
     Winds somewhere safe to sea.[14]

One must overcome the "divided-self," and become aware and experience this oneness of God. It is an awakening, an enlightenment that fosters an inner truth. When one reaches this spiritual state of consciousness, he learns and perceives many things he could not have understood in his human state of consciousness. The indwelling spirit beareth witness, because the spirit is Truth.

> In every person there lives an image of what he ought to be. As long as he is not that image, he nare at rest will be.
>
> Fredrick Roucart

As long as he is not that image, he will have substitute gods and as long as he does not elevate himself to a higher state of consciousness, he nare at rest will be.

In the creative evolutionary process we see the need to merge the separate-self with the Self. Those who choose to make an attempt to overcome their egotism will find their efforts aided by forces outside their conscious control. This force is an ungraspable movement from moment to moment within the melody of a divine dance.

There is but one Self which individuals realize as their source of existence: the eternal ground of infinite Being. Omnipotent, omniscient, and omnipresent. Beyond existence and non-existence, a Truth that lies beyond all concepts.

This Unity annihilates all separate entities. In this unity, duality and multiplicity disappear, and in this transcendental state of union, an unutterable source of existence pervades throughout the cosmos. At that moment you become aware of the source and fullness of the immortal and eternal spirit whose consciousness is not subject to time and space.

From this unity everything is born in whom we have our being, by whom everything is sustained, in whom everything resolves, and to whom we must return.

The failure of the mind to perceive, experience, and transcend the illusions of our assumed reality reduces the Self to less than what we are destined to be.

Such an awareness brings about an end to the finite world of time, space and matter, in which the concepts of duality (both subject and object) exist, to a consciousness of an infinite nature of nonduality where multiplicity ceases to be.

The individual who is aware knows that God-"Being," the conscious Self, is in everything and in this identity the individual and God are resolved, and the goal is reached.

The goal and the path are one.   Dogen

He lives in the infinite world of the eternal here and now, merging the Self in God, transcending all fears born of ignorance. If one fears that which is in the power of others either to deny or inflict, he becomes a slave.

Fear must be entirely banished. The purified
soul will fear nothing.

He who has found the bliss of the Eternal has
no fear from any quarter.

Upanishads

There are many ways to suffer, but only one way to live. It is not how you die that is crucial, but how you consciously live your life. Character is the label of the man, an index to everything he is and all that he will be. When all is said and done, if man does not have integrity, he has nothing.

Life has real meaning when we become aware and enjoy absolute freedom, "the pearl of great worth," while we are still in our bodies here on earth. In this state one acts completely through God.

Rise above the perception of the world, forget yourself and live in and by the vision of God. That vision is one of love that overcomes the fear of death of the mortal body.

> The world is a dream and death of the ego is the
> morning light.

When grasped, this understanding will save him from drowning in the sea of multiplicity.

> When I die, take me to where my love does lie
> and if she but give my cold lips a kiss, I shall
> again live for this.
>
> Jalahudlin Rumi

One is in truth the world and one is in truth immortal. All one has to do is die to his separated-self, and transcend the self-created beliefs of the mind to reach the real source of existence. To really live one only has to die.

> I know not how such things can be;
> I only know there came to me
> A fragrance such as never clings
> To aught save happy living things;
> A sound as of some joyous elf
> Singing sweet songs to please himself,
> And through and over everything,
> A sense of glad awakening.

I know not how such things can be!
I breathed my soul back into me.
Ah! Up then from the ground sprang I
And hailed the earth with such a cry
As is not heard save from a man
Who has been dead and lives again.

O God, I cried, no dark disguise
Can e'er hereafter hide from me
Thy radiant identity![3]

Behind one's ego burns the inextinguishable fire of Truth. Man himself-obstructs his own deliverance.

The egoistic mind harbors the misconception that it is capable of reviewing a book by looking at its cover, or by reading only one page and feeling qualified to render a review of its total contents. A word or a page must be understood or explained in terms of the whole. Words must be understood in the context of sentences, paragraphs, chapters, books, libraries, and life itself, a structure in which every brick derives its meaning only from its place in the whole. As in life, everything is dynamically interrelated, yet distinct.

If one is able to realize that he is not in spiritual reality separated, and that this separate-self is truly an illusion, then he understands that he, too, is eternally whole and that in spiritual reality he is not born or does not die.

Clearly, one's situation is paradoxical: being and non-being, eternity and death, whole and part. With deep intuition and not with thought, one becomes more and more aware of the universal mind and that one is in this world, but not of this world, and at the same time shares in immortality.

We must overcome our fears by detaching ourselves from the illusions of this world, so that our soul may merge and become united with the universal mind.

> The highest virtue whereby one may come most closely to God is absolute detachment from everything created.

True freedom consists in an interior detachment from everything created, to see beyond everything created and not be trapped by them. We must live our lives in the most complete manner possible and not let ourselves be tossed about as a leaf in the wind by the thoughts of an egotistical mind.

Detachment leads to where I am receptive to nothing except God. The purest form of detachment raises us above all desire and prayer. The detached soul does not wish for any reward from God, but only for God himself.

God's presence, if realized, will guide your journey in life. You will now exist in this world of multiplicity as a humble servant of God rather than a servant of an egoistic mind.

> As long as one feels that he is the doer, he cannot escape from the wheel of births.

Buddha

Man must go beyond his mind, forget his ego and act as an instrument of divine will. With this realization you will be in possession of all knowledge.

> The mind of the average human being is like a ship in which the sailors (senses) have formed a mutiny. They have locked the captain (God) and the navigator (soul) down below in the cabin and all the sailors feel the sense of complete freedom. One sailor, one part of the mind, steers for awhile, loses interest, leaves the wheel and another sailor, another part of the mind, comes up and steers for awhile.

The ship goes in circles. You feel free but real freedom consists in quelling the mutiny, bringing the Captain and the navigator up from below to take command again so that one can choose a goal and consistently and wholeheartedly with one's whole Being, steer towards it.

This ultimate breakthrough is the surrender to impermanence, the "letting go" of our ego, the merging of our separate-self with that ocean of tranquility, which is the ego-death that leads to liberation, the spiritual dimension of absolute freedom.

Death is the golden key that opens the palace of eternity.

John Milton

The realization of the true nature of the Self, which is identical with the ground of the universe, is the union with the divine principal of life.

Complete liberation, the immediate apprehension of the spaceless and timeless ground of Being, is possible even before physical death because the self is self-confined and there is no real embodiment for the Self to escape.

One must move from the separate-self as alienated consciousness to an awareness that all phenomena are a revelation of the same nondual ground of Being. The goal of the spiritual path is a nondual way of experiencing the world in which there is no distinction between subject and object.

Creation and becoming represent the disintegration of our primordial unity and the separating of the two forces of nature. In consequence man experiences a state of duality (subject-object) and in this illusion suffers "bondage."

So how can I set myself free?
Who has bound you?

Zen

No man can make another man a slave, unless that other has first enslaved himself. All dualism being illusory, there is nothing that really binds us, no chains to break, no freedom to attain. You cannot be separate from the whole and still call it the whole. Parts do not make up the whole either. Therefore, that which is whole, complete, and infinite can only be one, and it cannot be separate from anyone. Until you know this you remain in a state of duality.

> Just as each of us has one body with many members, and these members do not all have the same function, so in Christ we who are many form one body, and each member belongs to all the others.

Romans 12:4-5

One must be aware of the dualistic nature of the world and change his awareness in the way he perceives and acts in the world of opposites. Understanding himself as a part of the whole and, as such, completely submitted to the laws of the whole will naturally identify with all the other parts of the whole in a nondualistic mode of consciousness.

Knowledge is worth only what it yields in uplifting humanity to a higher spiritual state of consciousness, to a deeper understanding of God's purpose and man's destiny. Man's destiny is to evolve from the physical, material, and finite plane of existence to the Spiritual, creative, and infinite state of consciousness. The individual experiences his own Self-center, to be one with humanity's very Self.

Our task is to make the journey, transcend the self, and realize this final human destiny is to become one in

God consciousness. We must become aware of the God-, Christ-, Buddha-, Krishna-, or Mohammed-consciousness within us.

Christ and Buddha exemplify how compassion arises and manifests itself naturally when we have overcome our sense of separation. Human-consciousness is by nature the creative center of the finite universe. God-consciousness is by Grace the center of the infinite universe. God's grace is your foundation and will guide you on the spiritual way, lovingly lifting up your Being with a love that takes you inward and upward to the unutterable source of all existence.

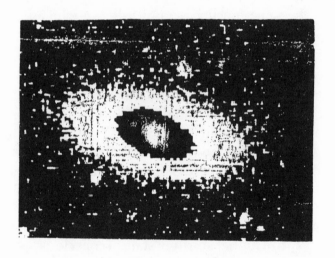

Self Purification

When we meet with the Self thus purified, even while here below, we have attained the heights, and need not further guidance.

Plotinus

Cravings and desires of the senses result in the manifestations of the seven deadly sins. Pride, laziness, greed, hate, lust, gluttony and envy-jealousy prevent man from unfolding to his true God-given nature. These are obstructions, and must be purified or eliminated in order for man to experience the kingdom of heaven that lies within and is the birthright of every individual. The mystical light of God shines forth from the soul that is purified. If man does not overcome these attachments, he dies unfulfilled.

So long as the heavenly expanse of the heart is troubled and disturbed by the excitement of desire there is little chance of our beholding therein the luminary God. The beatific Godly vision occurs only in the heart which is calm and wrapped in divine communion.

Did Satan, the power of darkness, cause the desire or did the desire invite the entering of Satan?

I only leave by the way I came in.   Satan

The Devil Complains

A sluggard once approached a fasting saint
And, baffled by despair, made this complaint:
"The devil is a highwayman, a thief,
Who's ruined me and robbed me of belief."
The saint replied: "Young man, the devil too
Has made his way here to complain—of you.
'My province is the world,' I heard him say;
'Tell this new pilgrim of God's holy Way

To keep his hands off what is mine—if I
Attack him it's because his fingers pry
In my affairs; if he will leave me be,
He's no concern of mine and can go free.'"[1]

"SIN" is the separation that prevents the inflowing of eternal life, which is the source of our individual being. In some way or other we have been cutting ourselves off from the Great Source of light, and what we want is to be reunited to it.

The afflictions of the soul cease when one has overcome the imperfections of the mind and its contaminations of the soul. Intense joy follows when the soul is purified and its fragrance remains for others to glorify in its presence. This state of perfection is salvation and exists in the perfect love of God.

Salvation is to be safe and happy in love and peace with all God's creation. The soul, when it is really at peace with itself, is at once united to God in love, truth, and beauty.

Love needs and desires beauty, and beauty
needs and desires love.

God so loved the world that He has given you that which is begotten (caused to exist) only of Him. He has given you this relationship, this oneness, this wholeness that can never be changed. Call it the Christ-, Buddha-, Mohammed-, or the Krishna-consciousness in you. It is the divine potential in everyone. The universal field of God.

To be in love is to surpass one's self. Love transcends all cravings and desires that are acting contrary to one's true nature of unconditional giving.

When one becomes victorious and conquers all of the seven deadly sins, he has come to full perfection. He has purified himself, so he will be able to experience the essence of God. When this essence of "Being" is experienced, all past regrets and future fears are canceled. Transcending, he is transformed and absorbed into the image and likeness of God by God's eternal grace. The destiny of the spiritual man is eternal life.

> Eternal life belongs to those who live in the present.
>
> Wittgenstein

Time is an illusion in life: the life of the past and future clouds men from the true life of the present. One must aim to destroy the deception arising from the past and future, the life in time. The true life is that now present to us, common to all, and manifesting itself in love. He who lives by love becomes, through the common life of all men, at one with God, the source, the foundation of life, the sum total of the laws in the fabric of nature. May our faults and errors of the past not hide the true life from us.

> Only those are truly free who have overcome
> the influences of their past.

Eternal life is a state of consciousness in eternal freedom, not bound by the desires of the mind, or harboring elements of the seven deadly sins. The state of eternal freedom is the way of life. At a time when mankind is yearning for freedom, it is important to point out that the way to external freedom leads over internal roads.

When the mind is forever under attack from within by our sexual and aggressive biological drives, as well as from without by parental, political, social, and religious ideologies, the soul becomes contaminated.

The mind, the intellect, leaves a man uncertain of the nature of the supreme reality without the direct experience. Every man is able to know for himself the truth of creation by a firsthand personal experience.

The experience releases the soul from the bondage of the material world and death.

We have a spiritual destiny beyond the material world. The call of conscience is the voice of God within us. The soul can never be truly human unless it is seeking God. We cannot escape it. It lives within us, throughout us, and seemingly beyond us.

When man has accepted, surrendered and totally submitted to the will of God, he will have transcended the mind-body duality to experience the fullness of creation.

> But you say, if he had wanted me to worship him, he would have left me some visible signs of his will. So he did, but you neglect them. Look for them; it is worth the effort.
>
> Pascal

> How do you know there is a God? You cannot see Him. Whose footprints do you see in the sand? They are the footprints of a camel. How do you know it is a camel? By the visible signs of its footprints. All we see around us are the visible attributes of God.

All acts of life are in harmony with the natural order of the universe. Man must overcome the desires of the ego that prevent the unfolding of the creative spirit from within. The man with even the merest trace of ego will see the Divine as existing outside of himself.

One must overcome the seven deadly imperfections completely. Any degree of one of these imperfections will prevent one from unfolding to his true God-given nature and experiencing the kingdom within.

> Your iniquities have divided you from your God.
>
> Isaiah 59:2

A hair's breadth of imperfections creates a deep gulf between heaven and earth. A woman that has just conceived might say that she is "a little bit pregnant." Either she is pregnant or not. She cannot be just a little bit pregnant. Either you are affected by a fraction of any one of these seven deadly sins, or you are not.

> For whoever keeps the whole law and yet stumbles in one point, he has become guilty of all.

By a little bit of imperfection you have become a transgressor of the whole law. One damns himself if he acts contrary to the natural law and order of the universe, and thus remains forever alienated from God.

Only those who have conquered the eternal enemy, the demands based in their childhood that interfere with their perception of reality, are truly free.

An unsatisfied need for love and affection in childhood results in the loss of innocence. The ego is dependent on its needs to be fulfilled by present external forces, as in childhood, and seeks them in the form of substitute gods and worldly gratifications.

> There are thousands hacking at the branches of evil to one who is striking at the root.

Thoreau

The oppressive emotions man experiences are rooted in the past. The soul is purified and free from its contaminations once the emotion is seen for what it really is, a distortion of an uncontrolled and misplaced sensation of the past. Once you become conscious of the cause of the emotion, you will be able to overcome its effect on you.

> A rock that is buried and cannot be seen is just as heavy as the one that is above the ground.

The very essence of divinity is a positive emotion of sublime love, a creative power of energy. The ultimate goal of love is to know that the reality of love is identical with the essence of God.

A purified soul in divine love is in communion with God Himself. It is the enthusiasm which can fire a soul and consume all that is within it. The individual then becomes one with the emotion, and he is never so thoroughly himself. He is simplified. He is unified. He is intensified.

There is a mystical power that can transform your life and will teach you all you wish to know. To discover this extraordinary power, this primal power of "Being," is the birthright of every individual. All you have to do is claim it.

We are always free to remake the self that seems to persistently plague our existence. Thus the man who declares, "I am what I am," is refusing to rise to the challenge of changing himself. He is saying "I choose to remain as I am." This is so sad.

The seven deadly sins are the sufferings and the pains associated with the isolation, frustration, fears, and separation from our divine nature. They are the beasts of creation.

He who fears has torment and is not made perfect in love. Fear is not of the present, but only of the past and future, which do not exist.

> Nothing real can be threatened.
> Nothing unreal exists.

How deceived was I to think that what I feared was in the world, instead of in my mind. We need reformers not of this world, but of ourselves. It is difficult to change others, but we can change ourselves.

> Most powerful is he who has himself in his power.
>
> Seneca

The redemption of man's soul is in the awareness of his transgression. If a man has done an evil act and is afraid lest he should become known, there is still a way of goodness in his evil. But if he has done a good deed and is eager that it be known, then even that good is a source of evil.

We have no hope of redemption from the seven deadly sins while the arrogant pride of ego remains, because pride prevents one from starting the journey to Self-purification.

> He said: "I went as usual—full of pride—
> Then saw a dervish by the highway's side.
> But then what happened next I can't be sure;
> My gold and silver went and now I'm poor!"
> They said: "Describe this man who blocked your way."
> He said: "I have; there's nothing more to say."[1]
>
> To glimpse this secret is to turn aside
> From both worlds, from all egocentric pride—[1]

Pride and sloth are the prime sources of all vices that prevent the soul's journey into a state of God-consciousness and participation in divinity itself. Pride because man is too proud to realize the need for the journey, and sloth (laziness) in pursuing the quest for Self-purification and the knowledge of Himself.

A sinner died, and, as his coffin passed,
A man who practiced every prayer and fast
Turned ostentatiously aside—how could
He pray for one of whom he knew no good?
He saw the sinner in his dreams that night,
His face transfigured with celestial light.
"How did you enter heaven's gates," he said,
"A sinner stained with filth from foot to head?"
"God saw your merciless, disdained pride,
And pitied my poor soul." the man replied.[1]

A man that has purified himself has humbled his pride, completed the journey, transcended the mind, and is one with the consciousness of God. He has found fulfillment derived from the omission of the seven deadly sins.

He is free from sexual and aggressive biological drives from within and the effect and restrictions placed upon him from without by society and his environment. He is free from parental, social, and political influences and religious ideologies that are the illusions of man's mind in the realm of time and space; so that the eight-fold paths of Buddha and the ten commandments of Moses are only by-products of his consciousness.

If you are led of the indwelling spirit, you are not under the law.

It is not in our power to control the actions of others, but it is up to us and in our power to decide if we are to let them linger within us and stir up our passions.

Man's enemies are his passions.

We should be in control of our passions, for when passions are in control of us they become vices and poison the soul. Man's passions cut him off from God. Passion unattended is a flame that burns to its own destruction. We must awaken the heart to compassion by the transformation of passion into compassion.

Everyone has desires. What counts is the way he handles those desires. We cannot prevent a bird from flying over our heads, but we can prevent the bird from building a nest in our hair.

> Thou shalt rule over thy desire.   Gen 4:7

Passions and desires are the enemies of charity. One that detaches himself from the senses achieves a mystical union with God. The kingdom of God on earth. The kingdom of God was, is, and shall be on earth; and he who makes an effort enters into it. The kingdom of God is in the soul of man. It is a cosmic union which unites all things on earth and in heaven.

Whoever seeks to unite himself with God from the depths of his soul will be absorbed into the heart of God. God will then fill him with humility, compassion, and love. A person's worth should be judged by the warmth of his heart, and through God man will know the reason for everything. Cosmic consciousness is the loftiest expression of man, the link that connects the visible to the invisible.

With cosmic consciousness the partial becomes complete, the crooked straight, the empty full, and the worn-out new. A religious or mystical experience is the realization of cosmic harmony, the expansion of the self until it embraces and merges with the whole; and, at the same time, contains the whole, where there is a complete union of body, soul and spirit, the natural, spiritual, and divine here on earth.

When we awaken to the reality of our being, a light begins to break upon us from within and we know the truth of "Being," and who we really are. This inner light enables man to become the object of wisdom. When he becomes aware that, "I am other than my body," he detaches himself from worldly interests and a direct revelation of God-consciousness takes place.

A purified soul is eternally present in God, and God is eternally present in all the objects of creation. There is nothing else apart from God, since all is in God. We are one with the spirit of the moment in life, death, and resurrection. This union of spirit triumphs over death, thus bringing about the full realization of the divine purpose in man.

Then let us seek perfection. Perfecting, purifying, maturing and refining is the aim of life. No matter how morally unworthy one has been, one's journey now is towards humility and how morally worthy one may become. Such a conception makes one severe in judging himself, and humane and compassionate in judging others.

The search for perfection, which is a search for divinity, is nothing more than the failure to accept our existence the way it is. One gets nearer to the heart of truth, the ultimate aim of the journey, in the measure that his mind ceases to struggle for perfection and surrenders and yields to the will and rhythm of the universe. A house divided against itself cannot stand. We must totally accept ourselves and others as we are.

> "Everyone is made perfect by God!" shouted the preacher. "Everything in the world is perfect!" he shouted again.
>
> After the sermon was over, a hunchback, stooped over, went up to the preacher and said, "If God made everything perfect, then why," pointing to his deformity, "am I a hunchback like this?"
>
> The preacher looked at him and smiled with grace and said, "Why, you are the most perfect hunchback that I have ever seen."

Happiness in our finite existence consists in being willing to be what we are. Completeness is not perfection; completeness is the acceptance of imperfections.

> When an enlightened person hears about Tao,
> He diligently practices it.
> When an uncertain person hears about Tao,
> He wavers between keeping it and losing it.
> When an unenlightened person hears about Tao,
> He treats it as a big laugh.
> If it were not just a big laugh to him,
> It would fall short of being the Tao.

Everyone's journey should be towards His perfection. We should seek to lay bare the precious pearl of man's spirit that is buried in all the imperfections of our existence. A precious pearl lies within you. One must penetrate its shell.

> Is the diver's interest in the shells or the pearls?

When God in His grace shows Himself to our soul, we have complete fulfillment. Fulfillment is when He is a host in our being. We no longer pray for anything, for our whole inner being is set in prayer, worshiping with such sweetness and delight that we can only pray in such ways as He leads us.

> Where He leads me, I will follow,
> I'll go with Him all the way.
> I can hear my Savior calling,
> "Take my cross and follow me."
> He will give me grace and glory,
> And go with me all the way.

Prayer and meditation is conditioning ourselves to experience God. For that which we seek is leading us.

> Sweet hour of prayer! sweet hour of prayer!
> That calls me from a world of care,
> And bids me at my Father's throne,
> Make all my wants and wishes known.

In seasons of distress and grief,
My soul has often found relief,
And oft escaped the tempter's snare,
By thy return, sweet hour of prayer.

Sweet hour of prayer! sweet hour of prayer!
Thy wings shall my petition bear,
To Him whose truth and faithfulness,
Engage the waiting souls to bless;

And since He bids me seek His face,
Believe His word and trust His grace,
I'll cast on Him my every care,
And wait for thee sweet hour of prayer.[11]

Those whose personal consciousness can perceive that the eternal life of the Spirit has been lost by the practice of the seven deadly sins will, by their renunciation, find freedom and build on the eternal foundation of Truth. God is the life of the spirit in men. He who lives in the life of the Spirit has infinite life. The spirit in us affirms that our life is eternal.

> The separation of Spirit and Soul from the mind and body of man is a death in consciousness.
>
> Ralph Waldo Emerson

Those who believe that a conscious death does not occur because of the practice of the seven deadly sins is building up a false hope of finding life after physical death of the body. He that is aware of the cosmic-universal conscious mind has eternal union of body, soul and spirit here on earth.

The religious life starts with humility and the awareness that we have once enjoyed a degree of perfection from which we have fallen, and the desire to atone for our transgressions. One comes to the realization that he is separated from this perfection by a veil.

When one sees through the veil of appearance and comes face to face with his (His) eternal identity, he realizes that the aim of human life is to become aware of his (His) divine nature. All religions are essentially in agreement, insofar as their message is derived from the teachings of those who have realized their own divinity.

The teaching of all genuine religious traditions is that our separate-self is but a flimsy charade, and what we really are is that one, bright, undivided consciousness whom most call "God." The Christ within, the Buddha which one Is.

Perfection is nothing but the union effected between God and the soul in perfect love. This is the love that springs from a pure spirit, free from all imperfections by the power of God's grace. If you are worthy, God alone bestows the grace of His wisdom on you. By His Grace we freely choose to love and serve him.

Lotus symbolizes flowering
of the human spirit

Faith

Faith is the substance of things unseen.

Meditation, like prayer and good works, should be done in secret. It is very difficult to pray to someone when you know so little about Him. We must rely on God solely through our faith. This faith is the acceptance, surrender, and loving submission to the will of God, pending confirmation.

It is imperative for those who have faith to truly believe and have confidence that their goal will be realized. It is to be realized only if it is based on trust and pursued with a pure heart and sincere intent.   An angelic state of purity.

> Then you will call upon me, and come and
> pray to me, and I will hear you.
> You will seek me, and find me; when you
> seek me with all your heart.

Jeremiah 29:12-13

Eventually one will come to the realization of true faith from the living experience, if he becomes one with the eternal process of life, whether he experiences the paradox as a drop of water returning to the ocean, or the ocean poured into the drop. In so doing he will individually experience the love and presence of God and gain the fruit of his labor. Enlightenment. The kingdom of Heaven. The kingdom that is of God. God as the ultimate and unique reality.

> Endure in love, be steadfast and sincere—
> At last the one you long for will appear.[1]

When confirmation is bestowed upon us and true faith is attained through our self-knowledge, patience and personal experience, then what once was a momentary experience is now abiding Self-knowledge. This Self-knowledge is both purifying and creative.

True faith now exists, a humble and patient submission to the will of God. It was attained by the realization of a living experience. Man's soul now has become one with the life and deeds of Christ-, Buddha-, Mohammed-, and Krishna-consciousness.

Our acceptance of this relationship and this love is made manifest by the concern we have for our environment and the way we treat the creatures of nature and act in relationship to our fellow man. There is only one consciousness in the universe and this consciousness is not only the source of all life, but life itself.

Faith and devotion are the preliminary steps to enlightenment. The initial step. The beginning of the quest. Faith is a believing attitude, it is a state of consciousness which turns on the Divine Flow that has always been present. If God exists, he exists because you perceive him to exist. God ceases to exist for those who cease to believe in Him. Belief is an assent to a credible proposition and one must believe in order to understand. In order for you to summon and experience His divine providence, you must invest part of yourself and your soul in the journey towards His presence.

> There is no god to us except he whom we have created in our own mind and having created him, who is to say he is not our God.

> Lynn Devries 16 years old.

> A little girl was crying because she had lost her doll. "If you stop crying I will buy you a new doll," said the father. "I do not want a new doll," cried the little girl, "I want my doll."

What the father did not realize was that his little girl had love invested in her doll and through this love, the little girl and the doll became one.

I and the Father are one.

John 10:30

Patience is the key to happiness. Only through patience does the fruit become sweet. Man is justified by his patience and glorified by his works, and not by faith alone. Faith without works is useless. For just as the body without the spirit is dead, so also faith without good works is dead. One's wisdom is seen by one's works.

For the Son of man shall come in the glory of his Father with his angels; and then he shall reward each person according to his works.

Matthew 16:27

God does not die when we cease to believe in Him, but we die when our lives cease to be guided by His radiant Presence, the source of which is beyond all reason.

Those to whom God has given religious faith by moving their hearts are very fortunate. They possess a true life in the present and the most glorious hopes for eternity. Those who do not have it can only acquire such faith through reasoned arguments, until God gives it by moving their heart with grace, without which faith is only human and useless for salvation. The heart has reasons that reason cannot know.

If any man would come after me, let him deny himself and take up his cross and follow me.

Matthew 16:24

A faith that God exists is a prerequisite for Grace. If we desire anything for its finite pleasure, we shall miss its infinite joy. God's celestial grace is only disclosed to those whose hearts are purified.

> Console thy self; thou wouldst not seek Me if
> thou hadst not already found Me.

Those who truly follow are prompted to do so by grace, and not by reason; and those who evade it are prompted by cravings and desires, and not by reason.

> Renew your courage, put aside your fear
> And in love's fire let reason disappear.[1]

An act of perfect sincerity, done for God's sake, might result in spiritual progress even though it might appear outwardly foolish.

Typical is the story of a not so very bright disciple whom some mischievous people teased, telling him that he would gain spiritual enlightenment by hanging himself by his feet from the roof and repeating some meaningless word they taught him. He followed their advice in sincerity and found himself illuminated the next morning.

The soul transcends reason, attains a direct experience of God, and is united with cosmic reality, where God ceases to be an object and becomes the experience.

The faith that will move a mountain is the faith needed to enable one to see beyond the ordinary world of illusion to the reality of cosmic-universal consciousness which is the essence of our existence. To gain this faith by experience one must perform the ultimate sacrifice, the death of the separate-self (ego). What empty foolishness it is to care for what must one day be dispersed to air.

This life's dim windows of the soul
Distorts the heavens from pole to pole
And leads you to believe a lie
When you see with, not through, the eye
That was born in a night to perish in a night
When the soul slept in the beams of light.

The Everlasting Gospel
William Blake

We must pursue the divine glimpses, those precious fleeting moments, the fleeting light of the divine Presence in the depth of our soul. Only then can we reach the point where we can grasp the wisdom of what faith truly is. Faith is certainty of conviction, independent from our perceptions and inferences. Faith cannot be given to man. The faith that stands on authority is not faith. Faith arises in man according to his inner experience and understanding.

Faith is the marriage of God and the Soul.

St. John of the Cross

It is a soul communion of the two-in-One. Our soul is eternally united to Him in love. He lives with the soul, and the soul dwells in Him. This is a marriage that gives and receives from life all its meaning.

Can the will of man resist the will of God's love forever?

Man's daily devotions are useless without sincerity. The sincere desire of the heart is always fulfilled by divine law. It is not so much something to be believed, as something to be lived. The most famous story illustrative of the single-mindedness of devotion is this:

"To love for love's sake."

Once, in the streets of Basra, Rabe'eh, a slave girl set free by her master, was asked why she was carrying a torch in one hand and a pitcher of water in the other, and she answered. "I want to throw fire into Paradise and pour water into Hell so that these two veils disappear and it becomes clear who worships God out of love, not out of fear of Hell or hope for Paradise."

If once in this world I win a moment with thee,
I will trample on both worlds, dance and be free.

Jalahudlin Rumi

Do not fear God, but fear that you will not find God, as a child who is lost has the fear of not finding his mother. The absence of God is Hell. To feel at one with God for a moment is better than all man's acts of worship from the beginning to the end of the world. A single speck of grace's shadow is better than a thousand efforts of the obedient servant. One can best worship God through love.

So I be written in the book of love,
I do not care about that book above.
Erase my name or write it as you will,
So I be written in the book of love.

Omar Khayyam

Abou Ben Adhem (may his tribe increase!)
Awoke one night from a deep dream of peace,
And saw, within the moonlight in his room,
Making it rich, and like a lily in bloom,
An Angel writing in a book of gold:
Exceeding peace had made Ben Adhem bold,
And to the Presence in the room he said,
"What writest thou?" The Vision raised its head,

And with a look made of all sweet accord
Answered, "The names of those who love the Lord."
"And is mine one?" said Abou. "Nay, not so,"
Replied the Angel. Abou spoke more low,
But cheerly still; and said, "I pray thee, then,
Write me as one that loves his fellow-men."

The Angel wrote, and vanished. The next night
It came again with a great wakening light,
And showed the names whom love of God had blessed,
And, lo! Ben Adhem's name led all the rest!

James Henry Leigh Hunt

Beloved let us love one another for love is of
God and everyone that loveth is born of God
and knoweth God.
1 John 4:7

Therefore let us love one another. Love is from God,
and every one who loves is the son of God, and knows
God. If we love one another God dwells in us, and we
dwell in Him. And he who does not love does not know
God, the light of Truth.

God is the source of all love, for love is an attribute
of God. His essence is beyond all attributes. Love
cannot be truly expressed in words. Love must be
experienced to be fully realized. The language of
experience become the language of love.

Blessed are the pure in heart for they shall see
God.
Matthew 5:8

Accept the indwelling spirit of pure love, and not the
conditions of the mind. Faith reaches the highest peak
of consciousness in the pursuit of God's love, and is
united in this love with God, the source of all perfection.
When the experience which was given by Grace has
passed and gone, then true faith prevails.

The holy books that were inspired by God, written and spoken by man, are merely interior road maps of experiences, drawn by people who have traveled them. Beliefs and creeds are only the means to an end and one should not be obsessed by the means. Belief is of the mind. Faith is of the spirit.

Wise men do not get involved with words.

This does not mean that we are forever to surrender conceptualization, provided we do not confuse the maps of reality with Reality itself. It is absolutely essential that man be able to tell the difference between a road map and the actual state of pure spiritual awareness.

A painted picture of a dumpling does not take one's hunger away. Pictures of food will not satisfy man's hunger and need unless the food becomes actualized. Neither will the words of God from all the holy books of the various religions in the world, with their particular set of beliefs and creeds, satisfy man's hunger and need for God unless they are experienced.

To study the Way is to study the Self. God in His love is calling to all to enter the path that leads to a higher state of spiritual consciousness and spiritual life. Love is the way of union with God, and the fruits of such love are the virtues of faith, hope, and charity. Faith in God, mankind and man himself; Hope in the victory over evil and the advancement of Humanity; and Charity in relieving the wants, and tolerant of the errors and faults of others.

We must travel the path to God ourselves, and other people's knowledge and wisdom will not aid us in doing so, except insofar as they point us in the right direction.

The immediate and intimate experience is like the lion who eats only what he himself has killed, as contrasted by the blind faith of the hyena who scavenges and lives on the remnants of other animal's prey. How sad it is to look at happiness through another person's eyes.

True faith is one with the fruit of enlightenment, the initial step to these various paths. And the fruit of enlightenment is one with faith, realized within the process of faith. If faith does not bear the fruits of enlightenment, then faith has not been realized. The experience cannot be fully realized unless the pilgrim, the initiate, seeks out a path with sincere intent and the faith of a pure heart that the object he desires and seeks does exist.

> It is love that asks, that seeks, that knocks, that finds, and that is faithful to what it finds.

> Saint Augustine

> Behold, I stand at the door and knock; if anyone hears My voice and opens the door, I will come in to him and will dine with him, and he with Me.

> Revelation 3:20

I wish that I were some beautiful land, called the land of beginning again, where all our mistakes, our heartaches, and our poor foolish pain, could be dropped, like a shabby coat, at the door and never put on again.

> Come, come again, whoever, whatever you may be, come:
> Heathen, fire-worshiper, sinful of idolatry, come.
> Come even if you broke your penitence a hundred times,
> Ours is not the portal of despair or misery, come.

> Abu Said Abu Khair

Just as I am, without one plea,
But that Thy blood was shed for me,
And that Thou bidd'st me come to Thee,
O Lamb of God! I come! I come!

Just as I am, and waiting not
To rid my soul of one dark blot,
To Thee, whose blood can cleanse each spot,
O Lamb of God! I come! I come!

Just as I am, tho' toss'd about,
With many a conflict, many a doubt,
With fears within and foes without,
O Lamb of God! I come! I come!

Just as I am, poor, wretched, blind,
Slight, riches, healing of the mind,
Yes, all I need in Thee to find,
O Lamb of God! I come! I come!

Just as I am—thou wilt receive,
Wilt welcome, pardon, cleanse, relieve;
Because Thy promise I believe,
O Lamb of God! I come! I come!

Charlotte Elliott

Faith, love, realization, and enlightenment interpenetrate each other so that without the initial effort of faith the others cannot be fully meaningful or realized. If love, realization, and enlightenment are not attained, one must question his motives and the sincerity of his faith to see if he were seeking it with a pure heart and pursuing it with sincere intent.

> God said, "It is not because he is despicable that I delay My gift to him: That very delay is an aid."

Softly and tenderly Jesus is calling,
Calling for you and for me,
See, on the portals He's waiting and watching,
Watching for you and me.

Time is now fleeting, the moments are passing,
Passing from you and from me;
Shadows are gathering, death-beds are coming,
Coming for you and for me.

Oh! for the wonderful love He has promised,
Promised for you and for me;
Tho' we have sinned, He has mercy and pardon,
Pardon for you and for me.

Come home, come home,
Ye who are weary, come home;
Earnestly, tenderly, Jesus is calling,
Calling, O sinner, come home!

Ancient Bible

God's Unconditional Love

The very structure of a paradoxical state lies
outside the human condition.

There was a man who had two sons; and the
younger of them said to his father, "Father, give me
the share of the estate that falls to me." And he
divided his wealth between them.

Not many days later, the younger son gathered
all he had and went on a journey into a distant
country, and there he squandered his estate with
loose living.

And when he had spent everything, a severe
famine occurred in that country, and he began to be
in need.

So he went and attached himself to one of the
citizens of that country, who sent him to his fields to
feed pigs.

And he was longing to fill his stomach with the
pods that the pigs were eating, but no one gave him
anything.

But when he came to his senses, he said, "How
many of my father's hired servants have bread enough
and to spare, but I am dying here with hunger!

"I will arise and go to my father, and will say to
him, 'Father, I have sinned against heaven, and in
your sight;

"I am no longer worthy to be called your son;
treat me as one of your hired servants.'"

And he arose and came to his father. But while he
was still a long way off, his father saw him, and felt
compassion for him, and ran and embraced him, and
kissed him.

And the son said to him, "Father, I have sinned
against heaven and in your sight, I am no longer
worthy to be called your son."

But the father said to his servants, "Bring quickly the best robe, and put it on him; and put a ring on his hand, and shoes on his feet; and bring the fattened calf and kill it, and let us eat and be merry;

"For this son of mine was dead, and has come to life again; he was lost; and has been found." And they began to be merry.

Now his older son was in the field; and when he came and drew near to the house, he heard music and dancing.

And he called one of the servants and began inquiring what these things might be.

And he said to him, "Your brother has come, and your father has killed the fattened calf, because he has received him back safe and sound."

But he became angry, and refused to go in. His father came out and entreated him,

But he answered his father, "Look! For so many years I have been serving you, and I have never neglected a command of yours; and yet you have never given me a goat, that I might be merry with my friends;

"But when this son of yours came, who has squandered your money on prostitutes, you celebrate by killing the finest calf we have on the place."

And he said to him, "Son, you have always been with me, and all that is mine is yours.

"But we had to celebrate and be glad, for this brother of yours was dead and has begun to live, and was lost and is found."

Luke 15:11-32

God's unconditional love is a gift. A gift is not a gift unless it is received. If you receive the gift, you will turn away from the sins that have been separating you from the will of God.

Grace comes to those, no matter how they've strayed,
Who know their sin's strength, and are afraid.[1]

The truth will be manifested unto you by the power of the Holy Ghost, and by the power of the Holy Ghost ye may know the truth of all things.

> If ye shall ask with a sincere heart, with real intent, having faith in Christ, he will manifest the truth of it unto you, by the power of the Holy Ghost.
> And by the power of the Holy Ghost ye may know the truth of all things.

Moroni 10:4-5

The Holy Ghost was simply a part of God which abided with Jesus, or any man after his union with God. Jesus believed he was the son of God, in precisely the same sense as he believed all men to be sons of God. Jesus personified the man who has recognized his (His) own divinity. The difference between him and other men, was simply this: that he knew he was the son of God, while they did not. The same heavenly Son in man must be lifted up.

It is not that God has responded to some and not to others, but that some have responded to God more than others.

> The Grace of God is like an ocean. If one comes with a cup he will only get a cupful. It is no use complaining of the stinginess of the ocean. The bigger the vessel the more one will be able to carry. It is entirely up to him.

Ramana Maharshi

Humility

> Whoever, therefore, shall humble himself as this little child, he will be greater in the kingdom of heaven.[15]

God's grace is sufficient to save all who seek Him. Our awareness of the pomp and vanities of this pretentious world in its empty affections and pernicious pride fosters, from the eternal ground of our being, humility, love, compassion, and social justice for all nature's kind. The loving goodness of God lies behind everything, and the recognition and acceptance of this fact is the secret of true humility. God is the divine origin of all that exists.

> The fear of the Lord is the instruction of wisdom.
> And before honor comes humility.

Humility is to see one's imperfections and humbly acknowledge them. A consciousness of one's faults is the seed to the humility that enables one to repent (a change of heart) and embrace humanity. Humility is the frank acceptance of all experiences. Humility is the mother of love and compassion, the awareness of all Truths.

Without humility one cannot have a change of heart and truly be humble. Humility is a work of the indwelling Spirit's mercy and grace. We need the light of grace to know our sins, weaknesses, faults and transgressions.

We can never attain the full knowledge of God until we have first known our own soul thoroughly and forgiven ourselves. We must forgive ourselves before we are able to forgive others and live in freedom, compassion, and love.

> To err is human, to forgive divine.

Only forgiveness heals. Blame keeps wounds open. With this forgiveness, our soul is moved to contrition and confession; then we are able to forgive the sins, weaknesses, faults, and transgressions of others. Mercy is exalted above judgment.

> God is All-forgiving, All-compassionate. God promises you His pardon and His bounty.

Quran

Before one can be forgiven, one must have suffered in order to become aware that his transgressions have separated him from his true God-given nature. If one repents one will be received and be granted forgiveness.

Be conscious of your faults and accept them without complaint, fear or reluctance but be aware of their consequences and realize that defending them is greater than the original offense itself because it is an offense against your soul. A vain person's inflated ego likes to prove it is right even when it is wrong. These faults or transgressions are separating him from his own original God-given nature, but their defense separates him even further.

> And Jesus went away from there, and withdrew into the district of Tyre and Sidon.
>
> And behold, a Canaanite woman came out from that region, and began to cry out, saying, "Have mercy on me, O Lord, Son of David; my daughter is cruelly demon-possessed."
>
> But He did not answer her a word. And His disciples came to Him and kept asking Him saying, "Send her away, for she is shouting out after us."
>
> But He answered and said, "I was sent only to the lost sheep of the house of Israel."
>
> But she came and began to bow down before Him, saying, "Lord, help me!"
>
> And He answered and said, "It is not good to take the children's bread and throw it to the dogs."

But she said, "Yes, Lord; but even the dogs feed on the crumbs which fall from their masters' table."

Then Jesus answered and said to her, "O woman, your faith is great, be it done for you as you wish." And her daughter was healed at once.

Matthew 15:21-28

It is my opinion that Jesus' divinity would not permit him to defend this prejudicial statement, "It is not good to take the children's bread and throw it to the dogs." That is paramount to saying, "It is not good to take the white man's bread and give it to the niggers."

When the Canaanite woman said, "Yes, Lord, but even the dogs feed on the crumbs which fall from the masters' table," she was acknowledging humbly that it was not important how she received the message; only that she receive it.

> Self-justification is worse than the original offense.
>
> Sheikh Ziaudin

Jesus' humility and compassion did not allow him to defend his offensive and disparaging statement and add to his offense. Jesus' divinity acknowledged his transgression and said, "O woman, your faith is great, be it done for you as you wish." Because faith was pure and sincere, the daughter was healed at once.

The damned must, in fact, deliberately harden their hearts to God in order to become damned. Sinners elect their Hell by an act of their own free will.

> For my omniscience paid I toll
> In infinite remorse of soul.
> All sin was of my sinning, all
> Atoning mine, and mine the gall
> Of all regret. Mine was the weight
> Of every brooded wrong, the hate

That stood behind each envious thrust,
Mine every greed, mine every lust.
And all the while for every grief,
Each suffering, I craved relief
With individual desire,—[3]

Agamemnon wanted to become a god. He struggled for perfection but in the end he was overcome and defeated by Apollo who then placed an earthly curse on him and all his descendents. The curse was that he and all his descendents would suffer because of his craving and desirous nature.

Agamemnon had a son named Orestes and the son was in a serious dilemma because his mother Clytemnestra had killed his father. Should Orestes avenge the death of his father as Greek society demands?

Although nothing could be more evil in Greek society than matricide, the killing of one's mother. What should he do? He finally gave in to the demands of others and killed his mother.

From that point on the gods inflicted suffering upon him that was unbearable. He suffered mentally and physically for the wrong that he had done. After suffering for many years, he prayed to Apollo and said, "Haven't I suffered enough?"

Apollo contemplated the circumstances and said that he would grant him a trial in which all the gods would be present. When all the gods were assembled, Orestes pleaded his case and said, "Haven't I suffered enough?"

Apollo interceded in behalf of Orestes and said that Orestes' father wanted to become a god. In that struggle Agamemnon did battle with Apollo and was defeated.

Upon defeating Agamemnon, Apollo placed an earthly curse upon him and all his descendents.

Orestes, being a descendent of Agamemnon, inherited that curse.

He related how he engineered it so that Orestes' mother would kill his father and that Orestes would then have to kill his mother.

Apollo pleaded with the gods that Orestes was not responsible for his actions because it was he alone that created the conditions that brought on the death of Orestes' mother.

Orestes quickly spoke up and said, "No, that is not what I am saying. All I am saying is, 'Haven't I suffered enough?'"

Upon hearing this the gods were astonished. Orestes was not blaming Apollo and the other gods for his crime of matricide or even blaming his parents for their actions but was taking responsibility for his own actions.

From that day forward the gods lifted the curse from Orestes and he was free. Orestes's nature now is one in harmony with that of the gods.

Ye shall know the truth and the Truth shall set you free.
John 8:32

Suffering is the parent of instruction, and the schoolmaster of life. The value of adversity and suffering is useful for those seeking self-development. Suffering is the means, selected by infinite wisdom, to purify the heart. One must not seek to lay the blame on others and bewail his fate. Only when we realize that our mistakes are of our own making will such disagreeable experiences free us from errors. We must first seek the errors within ourselves; and; through this introspection, the external obstacles become for us an occasion for inner enrichment and education. A heart free of prejudices is open to truth.

When someone else's failings are defined
What hairs you split—but to your own you're blind![1]

When one sees a fault in his neighbor, he should correct this very fault in himself; thus the mirror of his heart becomes increasingly pure. Those things which most disturb us in other people are really unrecognized aspects of ourselves.

Man stands in his own shadow and wonders
why it is dark.

It is the face of his own evil shadow that one sees and finds in others. We must be on guard against the faults we see in others. We should judge others only with great care and know that such carefulness begins with self-judgment. The wrong we have suffered that rouses our angry passions, we inflict onto others.

What you dislike in another take care to correct
in yourself.

Sprat

Rather than face our own faults we project them onto others, then convince ourselves and those around us that it is only they who are wrong. We should make a serious attempt to become aware of our own faults and not deceive ourselves by projecting them onto others. We first have to acknowledge that the evil with which we have to deal is within ourselves.

We are appalled by our own sins when we see them in others.

A Drunkard Accuses a Drunkard

A sot became extremely drunk—his legs
And head sank listless, weighed by wine's thick dregs.
A sober neighbour put him in a sack
And took him homewards hoisted on his back.

129

Another drunk went stumbling by the first,
Who woke and stuck his head outside and cursed.
"Hey, you, you lousy dipsomaniac,"
He yelled as he was borne off in the sack,
"If you'd had fewer drinks, just two or three,
You would be walking now as well as me."
He saw the other's state but not his own,
And in this blindness he is not alone;
You cannot love, and this is why you seek
To find men vicious, or depraved, or weak—
If you could search for love and persevere
The sins of other men would disappear.[1]

Are the greatest deceivers ones who deceive themselves?

We are upset at being deceived by our enemies, and betrayed by our friends, and yet we are often content to be deceived by ourselves.

Some even find comfort in deceiving themselves. It is we who possess the qualities that we dislike most in other people; and, if we can come to terms with ourselves, then we also will be able to come to terms with others.

You are standing in your own way.

There is none so blind as he who refuses to see.

Hypocrisy blinds a man to his own failings, making it impossible for him to experience the repentance, the total change of heart, that is necessary for forgiveness.

What you do speaks so loudly, I cannot hear what you say.
Ralph Waldo Emerson

You seem a sufi to common folk
But hide a hundred idols with your cloak.[1]

Only when one has repented and had a change of heart is he redeemed and able to forgive and to be forgiven. But he must be able to forgive himself before he is able to forgive others.

> If we cannot find contentment in ourselves, it is useless to seek it elsewhere.
>
> La Rochefoucauld

Physician, heal thyself!   Luke 4:23

Once you face the truth of your situation and see that truth for what it is, you can truly become free and open to new possibilities within yourself, and bring order into the chaos of your life.

> This above all: to thine own self be true,
> And it must follow, as the night the day,
> Thou canst not then be false to any man.[4]

He who knows himself also knows God. The sins of those sincere, repentance saves.

> You have forgotten who you are.

The knowledge of yourself as the very root, the very basis of creation, is the goal to be reached.

> Know thyself, and to thine own self be true.
>
> Socrates

It is impossible for a man to mount two horses, stretch two bows, or serve two masters. Otherwise, he will honor the one and offend the other. If you tie two birds together, even though they have four wings, they cannot fly. In the true essence of God as "Being," you must take responsibility for your own actions, ride your own horse, pull your own bow, and be your own master.

> Thou shalt prove how salty tastes another's bread and how hard a path it is to go up and down another's stairs.
>
> Dante

Peace of mind comes from not wanting to change others. True acceptance is always without demands and expectations. We must totally accept ourselves and others unconditionally.

> He who has so little knowledge of human nature as to seek happiness by changing anything but his own disposition will waste his life in fruitless efforts.
>
> Samuel Johnson

> The higher one climbs on the spiritual ladder, the more will he grant others their own freedom and give less interference to another's state of consciousness.
>
> Twitchel

In developing character man must take care not to become defensive and hardened in obstinacy, but to remain receptive to the consequences of his actions through strict and continuous self-examination.

> We must follow the example of the man who watches his Ox with a stick so that it will not graze on other people's meadows.

What is needed is not rigidity that holds fast to established principles and rules of order, but flexibility. One must evaluate and penetrate the circumstances of life from moment to moment to meet the needs of the time.

Islamic Prayer Mat

The Momentary Now in the Process of Existence

Today is Yesterday's Tomorrow

Reality includes past, present, and future, but existence includes only the present moment. Enlightenment does not reveal to us anything which happened in the past or which will happen in the future. Enlightenment is being caught up in the moment which is both in time and beyond time. Existence as we know it is a subset of Reality, which is unknowable.

Life is transitory and conditional to a perceived reality. Once our perception of opposites is transcended, the Now-moment brings about the awareness of immortality and eternal life. If realized, the total experience of the present moment is one with that of eternity, and eternity is one with the present moment.

The experience of immortality and eternal life is not a static thing to be achieved once, but something that grows with each effort, realized constantly in life from moment to moment with no thought of achieving an end apart from the means—the striving in the pursuit of worthwhile goals being the end in itself.

> Call nothing thy own except thy soul. Love not what thou art, but only what thou may become. Do not pursue pleasure, for thou may have the misfortune to pass it by.
>
> Man of LaMancha
> Miguel de Cervantes

The present moment determines the future, and the future has been determined by the past in the illusion of time and space.

> From beyond the finite the infinite comes and from the infinite the finite extends.
>
> Kabir

Here we have the finite world of "Becoming" and the infinite world of "Being." Being is an unchangable reality, eternally unmoved, that persists behind the deceptive world of incessant change.

One must not dwell on the past, and one must not have great expectations for the future; for the future has taken foot in the present. One must live in the present moment, learning not to be preoccupied with the past or the future. This allows one to perceive something previously unnoticed about the present moment.

> Take therefore no thought for the morrow, for the morrow shall take thought for the things of itself. Sufficient unto the day is the evil thereof.
>
> Matthew 6:34

Our todays and yesterdays
    Are the blocks with which we build.
Build today, then strong and sure,
    With a firm and ample base;
And ascending and secure
    Shall tomorrow find its place.

The conscious awareness of the present moment leads to a state of tranquility, a state of equanimity. This flight from the present moment ends when one is able to realize something about the here and now which does not change.

> There is no such thing as mortality, except the illusion, and the impression of the illusion, which man keeps before him as fear during his lifetime.
>
> Sufi mystic-Hazrat Kahn

If one does not live in the present moment, he sells his soul for a past regret or the hope of a future gain, he is separated from God's presence because he turns his back on Him.

The past has the ability to present "shadows of the things that have been." It does not judge, it cannot alter what has been. The future presents "shadows of things that have not happened but will happen" and lacks the power for reflection. This grim reaper cannot be diverted from its inevitable course. Only the present has the ability to comment on the events and to offer alternatives.

> Look not mournfully into the Past.
> It comes not back again.
> Wisely improve the Present.
> It is thine.
> Go forth to meet the shadowy Future,
> Without fear, and with a manly heart.

Henry Wadsworth Longfellow

Past, present and future are interdependent on the present moment. Love will unite one with all that is past, present, and future in one harmonious whole. The spirit of all three shall remain in our hearts forever. It is a momentary state of consciousness that is aware of all that exists, what has always existed, and will continue to exist. Just as the seed contains the past, present and future, everything that is, was, or will be was present before the Thought of Creation. The seed's activity in time arises out of its "Being," which is possessed essentially quite apart from time.

The seed is God's Word.   Luke 8:11

God is the sum of all parts, and all parts are the essence of creation. For God is all knowledge past, present, and future, and His creation is Spirit in form.

One who lives in the consciousness of God lives in the present moment, gaining eternal and inescapable union with his very Self. He has a life with the God-consciousness of past, present, and future events.

Where wert thou when I created the world?
Answer that and you have solved the riddle
of creation!

Job 38:4

Riddles are used as a theme for meditation. Riddles, like life itself, cannot be solved by any form of the intellect. Meditating on the riddle consists not of analyzing it, but completely merging with it, whereupon it solves itself. The exercise has one major aim, to merge the subject and object, and awaken the mind to the awareness and experience of God.

Creation is an eternal thought in the mind of God. Creation has come, evolved, and been caused to exist out of the pure consciousness of absolute "Being." God-consciousness opens every inner door. Spontaneity and elation underlies our infinite nature. In the spontaneity of the moment one becomes a co-worker with God. When we reflect on God's work and God's love in the revelations of our own goodness, our divinity imitates the source of that goodness.

The Great Way is not difficult for those who
have no preferences.

The Great Way is the mind of the universe. It is free and limitless like the limitless nature of parallel universes in quantum physics. The Great Way is what we make it. We must do something or not do it. There is no escape from the alternatives, infinite in number though they be. One of the infinite parallel worlds we choose of our own free will, will be our fate, our destiny.

Love leads whoever starts along the Way. One must simply listen to his inner Self, the essence of his (His) Being, to determine what he is to do and become, here and now, at this particular moment. Thus, life is a creative work of art, and the experience is the flowering of the soul—the soul becoming one with the spirit that IS.

What we are...is
God's gift to us:
What we become...is
our gift to God.

Creativity is a synthesis in which the dialectic play between opposites is temporarily suspended. Creativeness is not a continuous state; it is new from moment to moment as in the creative state of the artist. The present is a series of fleeting absolute Now-moments in the process of life that do not change, but successively fall away. Because the mind puts boundaries on life, we are unable to experience the present Now-moment as eternal, because the ego that the mind has created is in fear of its own death.

Tomorrow, she told her conscience,
Tomorrow, I'll try and be good.
Tomorrow, I'll think as I ought,
Tomorrow, I'll do as I should.
Tomorrow, I'll conquer the passions,
That keep me from heaven away.
Whatever, her conscience whispered,
One word and one only. Today.

Tomorrow, Tomorrow, Tomorrow,
And thus through the years it went on.
Tomorrow, Tomorrow, Tomorrow,
Youth like a shadow was gone.
Though age and her passions had written
A message of fate on her brow.
And forth from the shadows came death
With a terrible syllable—NOW!

Living and dying, birth and death, are simply different ways of viewing this timeless moment. Pure timeless awareness is independent of our birth and our death. The consciousness of the present moment never really ends. It only links the past and future.

All time is contained in the present NOW-moment. There is no time but NOW, and the only thing you ever experience is the eternal present. Past and future are One and the same. For is not the future forever passing into the past? Even this next little moment—now it's the past.

The present moment, which has come into existence, is just born and has no past behind it. The present moment which now dies, which has ceased to be, has no future. In the present moment birth and death are One. It comes into being and passes away at One and the same time. The only thing that is constant is change.

Life and death are not in conflict, they are some sort of dialectical unity. Birth and death are nothing but two different ways of viewing the reality of the present Moment.

In the absolute Present there is no past, and that which has no past is something which is just born. In the absolute Present there is no future either, and that which has no future is something which has just died; thus life, birth, death and eternity are one in this timeless present Moment. The veil between birth and death which obscures Reality is the same between past and future.

Man cannot be happy until he lives in the awareness of the present NOW-moment which holds within itself the complete sum of existence. Pile up enough tomorrows and all you will end up with is a bunch of empty yesterdays.

At each moment nature starts upon a long journey and at each moment reaches her end. All is eternally present in her, for she knows neither past nor future. For her the present is eternity. Our redemption is ultimately the resurrection of the soul, a release from the illusion of time—past, present, or future.

Because there is no past and no future outside the NOW-moment, there are no boundaries to this moment, nothing came before it, nothing comes after it. You never experience a beginning or end to it. The present moment is itself timeless, and that which is timeless is Eternal. To live one's life at each moment with full awareness is to live in the past and future at this moment. Eternal life belongs to those who live in the present NOW-moment.

> In this moment there is nothing which comes to be. In this moment there is nothing which ceases to be. Thus there is no birth-and-death to be brought to an end. Thus the absolute peace is this present moment. Though it is at this moment there is no boundary or limit to this moment, and herein is eternal delight.

> Platform Sutra

> The eternal now is a consciousness.

> Aldous Huxley

When man fears death, his ego refuses to live his life in the consciousness of the present moment. His fear of death compels him to pursue his favorite phantoms and to slay illusionary dragons that he perceives to exist.

A man at the ego level attempts to avoid the death of the timeless moment by living in a past that does not exist, and seeking a future that will never arrive.

> When you're on a journey and the end keeps getting further and further away, then you realize that the real end is the journey.[8]

To accept death man must live in the consciousness of the present moment devoid of time. The present moment is the only thing that has no end.

> The time of death is every moment. T.S. Eliot

Eternity is not an awareness of everlasting time, but an awareness which is itself totally without time. The eternal moment is a timeless moment, a moment which knows neither past nor future, birth, nor death. A non-dual awareness.

Silently and serenely one forgets all words;
Clearly and vividly That appears—
When one realizes it, it is vast and without limit;
In its Essence, it is pure awareness.
Singularly reflecting in this bright awareness,
Full of wonder in this pure reflection—
Infinite wonder permeates this serenity;
In this Illumination all intentional efforts vanish.
Silence is the final word.
Reflection is the response to all manifestation.
Devoid of any effort,
This response is natural and spontaneous—
The Truth of silent illumination
Is perfect and complete.

Hung Chih

The only Reality is the spontaneous activity of the present moment that knows neither past or future. Man is what he observes. He is the center of his universe. He knows the universe by being it. Eternity is present at every point of time, and infinity is present at every point of space. Therefore eternity and infinity exist in the consciousness of the present moment. The memory of the past and the expectations of the future exist only in and as the present.

In light of Eternity, past, present, and future are but one mystical moment in the Spirit and consciousness of God. God knows no past or future, but only an Eternal Now.

The eternity we seek has always been with us in our conscious awareness of God. For all that we need to do is to "let go, forget ourselves," and realize what we have always been. For life in the present "now" there is no spiritual death.

The life of the Creator and His creation are One that penetrates our whole being. This is a "momentary totality," which is perceived intuitively in a mystical now.

> Ah, my beloved.
> Come fill this cup,
> That clears today,
> Of past regrets
> And future fears.

> Omar Khayyam

There is no life until you have loved or been loved, for love transcends both time and space, fear, and regrets and exists wholly in the moment. Life is a free, ongoing essence of "Becoming." A free ongoing essence of "Being." It is the immortality of the spirit of man. There must be harmony of soul and body but we in our madness have separated the two. It is only love that will unite one with all that is past, present, and future in harmony with God and all His creation.

> Time was created so that everything would not happen at once.

The Reality of Truth, past, present and future is one and the same, existing somewhere beyond time and space, going beyond the paradoxical situations of life to be reunited, reintegrated in a state of absolute pure "Being," where God and man are and ever will be.

The grace of God resides in the present moment; and, by His Grace, we freely choose to love and serve him. The mind that dwells in the past or in the future has died to the eternal present. What is real is the consciousness of the present moment. It is a resurrection.

God-consciousness is a never-ending forward course of movement from moment to moment in the finite consciousness of life, death, and return (resurrection) of man and the universe to the source of all existence.

Universal salvation is completely realized in the here and now, and yet it is to be realized endlessly in the process of history. At each and every moment of history, a development toward the endless future is at that moment the total return to the root and source of history; that is, eternity is at that moment a development towards the endless future.

The process from moment to moment is not unlike that in the process of day, from dawn to sunset to dawn. No boundaries exist in the process of a twenty-four-hour day, but those the mind creates; so birth and death are part of the process of existence, even though we do not know what lies beyond death.

> All my life's a circle,
> Sunrise and sundown.
> The moon rose through the night,
> 'Til the daybreak comes around.
>
> All my life's a circle,
> I can't tell you why.
> Seasons spinning round again,
> The years keep rolling by.

Harry Chapin

Man moves from birth in the spring to summer ripeness, fall harvest, winter desolation, and death. Birth and death are a part of the cosmic cycle of life, as dawn to sunset are a part of the process of day.

The secret of immortality lies in seeing birth and death as an integral part of the cycle of life. Death is inevitable; accept it and life is affirmed. Immortality is the awareness from moment to moment of one's identity with the immortal process.

He said unto me "Write, for these words are faithful and true." And he said unto me, "It is done. I am Alpha and Omega, the beginning and the end. I will give unto him that is athirst from the fountain of the water of life freely. He that overcometh shall inherit all things and I will be his God and he shall be my son."

The Revelation to John 21:6-7

The ideal state of consciousness is to live in an "eternal present," outside of time, no longer possessing a personal consciousness but a witnessing consciousness, which is the awareness of a non-conditional existence of pure spontaneity, a paradoxical state of nonduality, the inexpressible experience of Unity.

This paradoxical condition is obtained by "death" to the human condition and "rebirth" to a transcendent cosmic-universal state of being—a life more real by the incorporation of the sacred.

Man must transcend the phenomenal world of opposites, from duality to nonduality, and pass into that unconditioned and timeless state in which opposites cease to exist, where there is neither day nor night, birth nor death, and attain the paradoxical truth of God and His wisdom by becoming conscious that the ultimate nature of the phenomenal world is identical with that of God.

> You are His shadow, and cannot be moved
> By thoughts of life or death once this is proved.
> If He had kept His majesty concealed,
> No earthly shadow would have been revealed.[1]

It is a "rebirth," a cosmic reintegration of the soul to a state of "supreme bliss" that preceded creation. By means of a personal experience man gains immortality by experiencing his own death and resurrection while still in his body.

The world has never known a state like this,
This paradox beyond analysis.[1]

My perception of the second coming of the Messiah, the deliverer, is allegorically represented as the spiritual second coming of Christ. The resurrection is the anointment and consecration of man's soul into Christ-consciousness. The spiritual experience is the "rebirth" of man's soul into the heart of God.

Truly, truly. I say to you, unless one is born again, he cannot see the kingdom of God.

John 3:3

Man is spiritually reborn again and becomes as a little child that existed before the separation. The way of spiritual childhood is the path which leads to eternal life.

Truly, I say unto you, unless you change and become like little children, you shall not enter the kingdom of heaven.

Matthew 18:3

Knowledge is of little value as long as it is not realized in a personal experience. Experience then is indispensable for salvation for one sees the soul in all beings, and all beings in God.

To him who sees me in everything and everything in me, I am never lost, and he is not lost in me.

Being one he becomes many, or having become many becomes one again.

Initiation, death, and mystical resurrection is a rebirth to another mode of Being. It is a continuous process of becoming, dying, and being reborn again.

If one had proceeded from Unity to multiplicity, he would like-wise return at the end from multiplicity to Unity. Alpha to Omega to Alpha again.

The fear of death will no longer drive man to folly, waste and destruction, and he will live in the infinite moment by living fully in the "now" of experience.

> Jesus and Buddha say that if you cling to life you will miss it.

> Seek no happiness for fear of passing it by.

> Life is like a railroad station. The train of birth brings us in. The train of death will carry us away.

Life, from birth to death, is little more than one precarious breath. If we can live with the knowledge that death is our constant companion, then death can become our ally, a continual source of wise counsel. With death's counsel, the constant awareness of the limits of our time to live and love, we can always be guided to make the best use of our time and live life to the fullest.

God is actively nurturing us so that we might grow up to be like Him. He brings us face to face with the grandeur of our destiny, so that we might become a new life form of God.

> I give Him also life by knowing Him in my Heart.

Man must be in harmony with the earth as the earth is with heaven, and heaven with the supreme way, and the supreme way is the way it is. Man must live in harmony and oneness in God-consciousness. The law of eternal harmony is the truth of Being. The truth of Being brings love, peace, and harmony out of all discord.

At every single moment of one's life one is what one is going to be, no less than what one has been. One can fully attain this perfection from the ultimate realization of Self-development.

He is able to observe the waxing and waning of life in this world, while abiding unassertively in a state of unshakable serenity. To achieve this cheerful serenity is a virtue. The finest and highest of human endeavors. Such cheerfulness is supreme insight and love, affirmation of all reality. This is how the source of all existence expresses itself.

Olive Branch

How calmly does the olive branch,
observe the sky, begin to blanch.
Without a cry, without a prayer,
with no betrayal of despair.
Sometime, while the night observes the tree,
the zenith of its life will be
gone past forever, and from thence,
a second history will commence.
A chronicle, no longer gold,
a bargaining with mist and mold.
And finally the broken stem,
the plummeting to earth and then,
an intercourse, not well designed
for beings of a golden kind,
whose native dream must arch above
the earth's obscene corrupting love.
And still the ripe fruit and the branch,
observe the sky, begin to blanch.
Without a cry, without a prayer,
with no betrayal of despair.
Oh! courage, could you not as well
select a second place to dwell.
Not only in that golden tree,
but in the frightened heart of me.

Tennessee Williams

Just sitting, doing nothing, the spring comes and the grass grows by itself. You are simply relaxing into your own being, not doing anything at all. It is not a question of doing; it is simply a question of Being.

In this moment there is nothing which comes to be. In this moment there is nothing which ceases to be. Thus there is no birth-and-death to be brought to an end. Wherefore the absolute tranquility in this present moment. Though it is at this moment, there is no limit to this moment, and herein is eternal delight.

A moment comes when you are in your utter purity, in your utter simplicity, in your utter innocence. In the Now-moment, past and future fall away. It is through this simplicity that the precious pearl of His spirit is revealed.

It is as though he were blind and deaf. Seated in his hut, he hankers not for things outside. Streams meander on of themselves, red flowers naturally bloom red.

When the curtain of time that hides us from tomorrow is drawn, there are openings through it which give us glimpses of eternity. In order to realize God, nothing needs to be gained or added; an obscuring curtain needs only to be removed.

As a Zen master was fanning himself, a monk came up and said: "The nature of the wind is constance. There is no place it does not reach. Why do you still use a fan?" The master answered: "You only know the nature of the wind as constance. You do not know yet the meaning of it reaching every place." The monk said: "What is the meaning of 'there is no place it does not reach'?" The master only fanned himself. The monk bowed deeply.

It is the wise man who lives in harmony with the Divine will, and it is the fool who brings disaster upon himself. Love is the transforming and also the reforming element of life that transforms all discord into harmony. Love can transcend all desires that are the cause of the seven deadly sins, and transform the raging destructive lion of hate into the harmless lamb.

The Zen master Hakuin was praised by his neighbors as one living a pure life.

A beautiful Japanese girl whose parents owned a food store lived near him. Suddenly, without any warning, her parents discovered she was with child.

This made her parents angry. She would not confess who the man was, but after much harassment at last named Hakuin.

In great anger the parents went to the master. "Is that so?" was all he would say.

After the child was born it was brought to Hakuin. By this time he had lost his reputation, which did not trouble him, but he took very good care of the child. He obtained milk from his neighbors and everything else the little one needed.

A year later the girl-mother could stand it no longer. She told her parents the truth—that the real father of the child was a young man who worked in the fishmarket.

The mother and father of the girl at once went to Hakuin to ask his forgiveness, to apologize at length and to get the child back again.

Hakuin was willing. In yielding the child, all he said was: "Is that so?"

Life depends on polarities, the polar oppositions of the changes inherent in the process of life. The divine state is gained by he who realizes in his own body the union of the two polar principles. The exhaustive penetration of these diversities depends upon the spirituality and clarity in the perceptive individual. These two fundamental forces serve to explain all the phenomena in the world. In the center of these interacting forces is the spirit.

Spirituality

All around are dualities of life,
All around are Yin Yang of strife,
The spirit lies within.[9]

Love is the way, the truth and the light.

The Truth is the end and aim of all existence, and the world was created so that the Truth could come and dwell therein. Those who fail to aspire to the Truth have missed the purpose of life. The purpose of man's creation is to reveal and experience the Divine Presence in this world, and to know God with all his heart through the path of love.

Blessed is he who rests in the truth.

Buddhist saying

We live in a world of opposites because, we do not accept the world as it is. We put boundaries in life; and, if we are able to transcend these boundaries, then life has served its purpose.

The core and essence of one's being is perfect love in a sea of tranquility. To experience the sea of tranquility is to see opposites as complementary rather than contradictory. It is a changeless essence in the ever-changing creative evolutionary process in time and space. The only aspect of time that is eternal is now.

Some forfeit eternal bliss for the sake of a passing gain.

The purpose of man's life is Self-development: to seek God so that he (He) could be known, and realize his

(His) nature perfectly—to be One, moment to moment, with the process of existence.

One must start living his (His) existence from moment to moment. Existence is not in the past or future, but in the present, here and now. Life is an infinite succession of nows when you become the very essence of whose existence is ceaseless change. The meaning of life and being alive is to lose your separateness of Being and experience the absolute freedom and spontaneity of the moment. The spontaneity of the moment is "Being."

We are indeed bathed in God's "Being" as fish who swim in the ocean are bathed in the ocean.

> A fish went to a queen fish and asked: "I have always heard about the sea, but what is the sea? Where is it?"
>
> The queen fish explained: "You live, move, and have your being in the sea. The sea is within you and without you, and you are made of sea, and you will end in sea. The sea surrounds you as your own being."
>
> Hindu story

We, like fish in an ocean, swim in an ocean of divine grace. Our spiritual journey is waking up to the divine sea in which we swim.

A pot filled with water and submerged in the water of the ocean is full inside and out. Thoughts come and go, objects of thought come and go, but conscious awareness is not affected. No object stands apart from me, just as the ocean is not divided by the walls of the submerged pot; and, as a drop of water that knows it is water can say, "I am the Atlantic and the Pacific."

The awareness of a consciousness pervading everywhere and encompassing everything is a deeper experience of merging with that consciousness and realizing that it is "my" consciousness, whereupon even the last trace of duality disappears.

The way to lasting peace, success, and happiness lies in apprehending and giving actuality to the way of the universe and becoming one with the other person. To become one with the other person is to become one with the essence of life.

> One should always endeavor to succeed with the help of others rather than at the expense of others.

The course of the creative evolutionary process alters and shapes our soul until we attain our true nature in conformity with the conscious harmony and natural order of the universe. This creates order out of the chaotic changes in the evolutionary process of life.

> You must have chaos within you to give birth to a dancing star.
>
> Nietzsche

Our whole life is a challenge to spiritual growth, and the process of spiritual growth is self-unfoldment. Life's processes are lessons in spiritual evolution, and this life is a passing phase in the soul's progression toward perfection.

All things are forever changing but nothing dies. Death is only a boundary that man puts on the process of his existence. We must eliminate the boundaries that separate appearance from Reality. Man passes in a whisper on the edge of eternity, and his soul within human form wanders through change. Clouds of ignorance overshadow the light of Truth. Time devours all things in the process of life and is itself a constant movement from moment to moment in the process of renewal, like a well of water springing up into man's everlasting life, clear as crystal, coming from the throne of God, the tree of life.

I will pour out My Spirit on all mankind; And
your sons and your daughters shall prophesy,
your old men shall dream dreams, your young
men shall see visions:

Joel 2:28

Our life flows by like water in a river or like sand in
an hour-glass. We are not matter only, but a spirit that
dwells in the heart of God. Time has no power except
that over the body. The body transcends matter, and the
mind transcends the body. In meditation the soul
transcends the mind, then the Spirit transcends the soul.
The Spirit of God is part of us, and we are a part of it. The
Spirit is the better part, immortal and existing before
and beyond time.

God is the created universe as mind is to a
body.

Ramanuja

The only consistence in the universe is that the
universe remains in constant change, one of movement
and growth from moment to moment in the creative
evolutionary process. Within this sphere of time and
space, its constant change seems to revolve, to circle
round one center.

My joy, my grief, my hope, my love did all
within this circle move.

There are physiological changes in the human body;
every tissue, every cell changes a number of times in
one's lifetime, but the true essence of the person remains
the same.

Underlying the exterior world of change is an
unchangeable reality, which is identical with that which
underlies the essence of man. God's union is realized
during periods of grace and in the process of meditation.

The center of all existence is the cosmic-universal mind. It is there that one knows the nature of his own being and becomes whole. All movements, thoughts, and words emanating from the center are attributes of Truth. In the center one is free from the passions of the senses and all external things seem gradually to lose their hold on him, while the soul, on the other hand, regains its lost control.

When one experiences this center, even for a few moments, everything concerning the nature of the cosmic-universal mind will at once become clear and no further explanation will be necessary. One is fortunate if he experiences an initiation that exposes him to the realization that one's journey now is to return to the center. He has then had a personal transcendent experience with the Divine. In the study of Zen Buddhism this type of realization is known as "sudden enlightenment." In the study of Christianity it is known as "Grace."

Nothing except God exists. The whole universe, including man, is essentially one in God—whether it is regarded as an emanation which proceeds from Him without impairing His unity, like sunbeams from the sun, or whether it is conceived as a mirror image in which the divine attributes are reflected.

> Do we perceive the universe or are we an extension of the universe?

The sun represents God and is forever giving off light. The moon is like man reflecting the light of that which is God. When the earth, represented as the ego, obstructs the light of the sun, the moon is then plunged into darkness.

God's will, reflecting through the mind, produces out of itself the visible world and all within it. God is immanent in all created things. He is one with the world in those choosing to follow Him.

He has no separate existence outside of them except for those attributes which He does not share with the world, such as His limitless nature, rule, and guidance.

When a separate existence is perceived by the mind, the ego becomes prevalent, obstructs the will of God, and plunges man into darkness.

We live in either a finite consciousness in which the ego perceives itself as the center of the universe, or an infinite awareness that transcends time and space and lives in the spontaneity of the present moment as part of the creative evolutionary process of existence.

In Taoism the primordial one becomes two in creation; then two becomes three, and so on, in ever increasing numbers. The ten thousand things that represent the uncountable arise from the Tao, containing all possibilities within the multiplicities of the world.

> The Taoist first transcends worldly affairs, then material things, and finally even his own existence. Through this step-by-step non-attachment he achieves enlightenment and is able to see all things as One.

> Chang Chung-yuan

Wisdom sees through all illusions. It releases you from your bondage and frees you from all desires. You are no longer a slave to your passions. You are beyond the sphere of relative consciousness, which is in the realm of the ten thousand things. You are at the very center, which sustains the entire system of multiplicity.

> Being at one with the Tao is eternal. And though the body dies, the Tao will never pass away.

> Tao Te Ching

The nameless is the origin of heaven and earth. Naming it is the mother of ten thousand things (our perceived reality). The world is made up of ten thousand things, and each one of them cries out to us absolutely nothing. We sit in the circumference and suppose, and the Truth sits in the middle and knows. The circumference is the ten thousand things.

> God is an intelligible sphere whose center is everywhere and whose circumference is nowhere.
>
> Hermes Trismegistus

God and His Love are the center of a circle without a circumference.

> The mind has one thousand eyes;
>   And the heart but one;
> Yet the light of the whole life dies
>   When love is done.

Man's prior nature is Spirit, the Ultimate Whole, but until he discovers that wholeness, his mind will remain an alienated fragment and in fear and terror of death. Time was created by the repression of death. When mind soars in pursuit of the things conceived in time and space, it pursues emptiness. But when man dives deep within himself, he experiences the fullness of Being—the immediate apprehension of the spaceless and timeless ground of Being.

The Hindus say that the mind that sees and divides the whole into the ten thousand things must die, and one must go beyond the mind to experience his (His) center. To find out what is real, you have to go beyond the creations of the mind, and in this stillness there comes into being love, truth, and beauty.

> For one whose mind is ready, I am easy to know.

The mind is the ten thousand things in time and space. Suffering only comes into the world with the advent of the ego and the ego experience. The mind creates the suffering by dividing the whole into ten thousand things, and only by an elevated state of consciousness will one comprehend and experience the fullness of existence. The world is multiplicity, not consciously lived as one in God.

> Heaven and earth and I
> are of the same root,
> The ten-thousand things and I
> are of one substance.
>
> Sojo

When one's soul looks to find his destiny outside of himself, in the ten thousand things, the circumference, the sphere, the mind, multiplicity, he will discover and experience himself as only a part of a magnificent whole, and will never come to the realization that a synthesis could occur that would unite his soul with that of God.

> I laugh when I hear that the fish swimming in
> the water is thirsty.

To those who never experience the journey, they may find it difficult to accept God as "Being." Man is either caught up in his perceptions of the world and its ten thousand things or is one with the essence of his (His) existence.

> One fish in a fish bowl said to the other, "If you
> don't believe in God, then who changes the
> water everyday?"
>
> Kabir

One must look within himself to find this synthesis. An unexamined life is not worth living. When one reaches this spiritual state of consciousness, then he learns and understands many things he could not have understood in his human state of consciousness. Everything is interrelated, and all are expressions of cosmic-universal consciousness.

> For him who has perception, a mere sign is enough. For him who does not really heed, a thousand explanations are not enough.

Haji Bektash

Jesus said, "Blessed are the poor in spirit for theirs is the kingdom of Heaven." Buddha said, "Blessed are those who do not crave or desire, for they shall experience their true Self." Poor in spirit is an emptiness of the ten thousand things, which include cravings and desires. When there is emptiness, that emptiness is what Jesus calls the kingdom of heaven, and Buddha calls Nirvana.

> The kingdom of heaven is like a treasure hidden in a field, which a man has found and covered up; then in his joy he goes and sells all that he has, and buys that field and gets the treasure too!
>
> Matthew 13:44

This field is the soul wherein the treasure of the kingdom of God lieth hidden. In the soul, therefore, are God and all creatures blessed.

> The kingdom of heaven is like a merchant in search of fine pearls. When he found one of great value, he went and sold all that he had and bought it.
>
> Matthew 13:45-46

Truth is a pearl of great worth that is found at the center of one's conscious being, while at the circumference all things are falsely accepted by the consciousness of a collective-social order—a social order that views oneself through the attitudes of others.

The problems in relationships come because people are living in the circumference. In the circumference the mind and senses are stirred up to distract the tranquil life at the center. This unifying center is consistently under attack by the forces of heredity as well as the actions of the mind and the senses. It is a battle between flesh and spirit.

> What a mighty fortress of peace, what a bastion
> of strength the center really is.

The quest for union takes the form of a journey towards God. It is to experience the love that will enable you to gain insight into the mysterious force able to contain the boundlessness of all creation and realize that the object of one's desire is not of this world.

> There is a den in you where dragons thrive;
> Your folly keeps the prowling beasts alive.[1]

One must detach his consciousness from this world to gain independence and serenity. Once detached from all finite worldly passions and desires, he becomes aware of his unity with the whole. He becomes bewildered and in awe of its magnificent splendor and, thus, finds peace and fulfillment in the heart of God.

> Behind every dragon there is a treasure; all one
> has to do to acquire the treasure is to slay
> (transform) the dragon.

Man has lost sight of that inward process. Once the soul is separated from its true Self, it suffers; and it becomes necessary to go through many trials and tribulations before it journeys home to its center.

Trials and tribulations are all necessary stages of purification through which man is delivered from attachment to himself and the world—to find the place he was seeking—to find the place he had never left. The Self cannot be attained; it must be realized.

Man's destiny is within himself, the Self that knows in unity all truth, before whom all past and future truth is clear in one eternal moment.

We do not have to seek God, for God is always with us here and now, at this very moment. He leads us to realize the folly of our actions and to turn to wisdom; wisdom that can be gained from suffering.

As they sinned so are they punished.

Man must persevere until he journeys to, into, and through the heart of God.

I steal by lawn and grassy plots, I slide by hazel covers.
I move the sweet forget-me-nots, that grow for happy lovers.
And out again I curve and flow, to join the brimming river.
For men may come and men may go, but I go on forever.

Tennyson

Lotus is legendary wellspring of god Brahma the Creator

Transcending Good and Evil
A matter of perceptive awareness

The atheist does not believe in the existence of God. The agnostic believes it is impossible to know whether there is a God or a future life. Some believe that life has no meaning and is senseless and useless.

> Life is a tale told by an idiot,
> Full of sound and fury, signifying nothing.[4]

Everything in existence may be false or true depending upon our perception. There is no God! Or is there? Life is senseless and useless! Or is it?

Hamlet

To be, or not to be,—that is the question:—
Whether 'tis nobler in the mind to suffer
The slings and arrows of outrageous fortune,
Or to take arms against a sea of troubles,
And by opposing end them?—To die,—to sleep,—
No more; and by a sleep to say we end
The heart-ache and the thousand natural shocks
That flesh is heir to,—'tis a consummation
Devoutly to be wish'd. To die,—to sleep;—
To sleep! perchance to dream:—ay, there's the rub;
For in that sleep of death what dreams may come,
When we have shuffled off this mortal coil,
Must give us pause: there's the respect
That makes calamity of so long life;
For who would bear the whips and scorns of time,
The oppressor's wrong, the proud man's contumely,
The pangs of despiz'd love, the law's delay,
The insolence of office, and the spurns
That patient merit of the unworthy takes,
When he himself might his quietus make
With a bare bodkin? who would fardels bear,

To grunt and sweat under a weary life,
But that the dread of something after death,—
The undiscover'd country, from whose bourn
No traveller returns,—puzzles the will,
And makes us rather bear those ills we have
Then fly to others that we know not of?[4]

God is present everywhere and absent only from those unable to perceive him. Our self-importance separates us from God. The separation is our punishment, not unlike a miser who leaves this world without knowing the truth about himself. When we do perceive Him, we have another life.

A miser died, leaving a cache of gold;
And in a dream what should the son behold
But his dead father, shaped now like a mouse
That dashed distractedly about the house,
His mouse-eyes filled with tears. The sleeping son
Spoke in his dream: "Why, father, must you run
About our home like this?" The poor mouse said:
"Who guards my store of gold now I am dead?
Has any thief found out its hiding-place?"
The son asked next about his mouse-like face
And heard his father say: "Learn from my state;
Whoever worships gold, this is his fate—
To haunt the hidden cache for evermore,
An anxious mouse that darts across the floor."[1]

For what shall it profit a man, if he shall gain the whole world and lose his own soul?

Mark 8:36

Man's destiny, they say, is written in the stars—all he'll ever do, all he'll ever love, all he'll ever be; and, once written, they say, it can never be changed. If this be true as I now suppose it must, then only one question remains. Who does the writing? If I knew the answer to that, if I could be sure, then I would know whether to curse God for what my life has been or praise the devil.

Those who go beneath the surface do so at their peril.

Oscar Wilde

They will be gone, lost forever unless they transcend the world of opposites and realize that their suffering is self-inflicted by their perception of Reality and by the choices they make.

All opposites are mutually interdependent and inseparable, non-dual. He who imagines otherwise does so at his own peril.

> Is there a difference between yes and no?
> Is there a difference between good and evil?
> Must I fear what others fear? What nonsense!
> Having and not having arise together
> Difficult and easy complement each other
> Long and short contrast each other
> High and low rest upon each other
> Front and back follow one another.

Tao Te Ching

There are forces in the universe, created for good, but which may serve for evil. Those who say that they would have right without wrong, or good without evil, do not apprehend the great principles of the universe, nor the nature of all creation. One might as well talk of the existence of Heaven without that of Earth, or of the negative principle without the positive, which is clearly impossible.

Light and darkness are the world's eternal ways. Evil, wrong, and suffering are temporary. They are necessary to the mighty chord that makes the apparent discord one of perfect harmony. Evil is merely apparent; all is in reality good and perfect. For pain and sorrow, persecution and hardships, affliction and destitution, sickness and death are the means by which alone the noblest virtues could be developed. Without them virtue would have no existence, above which none of the lofty elements of human nature would emerge. We must know evil—our own capacity for evil—before we are capable of good.

> Throw away Thy rod,
> Throw away Thy wrath;
> O my God,
> Take the gentle path.

Now there are diversities of gifts, but the same Spirit.

And there are differences of administrations, but the same Lord.

And there are diversities of operations, but it is the same God which worketh all in all.

But the manifestation of the Spirit is given to every man to profit withal.

1 Corinthians 12:4-7

All that is true, by whomsoever it has been said, is from the Holy Spirit.

St. Ambrose

There is no absolute right or wrong, good or evil in this relative world, but only the experience and the way one perceives it, where two contradictory statements can both be true, where the course that events take depends on their subsequent perception.

Life is a comedy of errors. Comedy or tragedy? Good or Evil? Is it a matter of perception?

When evil finally becomes insufferable, it may touch its point of cure. If by suffering, the soul discerns the truth and becomes aware and conscious of its finite nature and of its infinite existence then evil must be perceived as good, and beyond the paradox is the way-to-Truth.

The truest sayings are paradoxical.

Taoism

Long ago, in a village far away, there lived two brothers who were as different as two people could possibly be. In fact, you could search the whole world over and be unlikely to discover two young men with so little in common. For whereas the elder was studious, the younger cared nothing for books and learning; and while the elder was courteous, the younger tended to be quite rude; and though the elder ate and drank moderately, the younger ate gluttonously and drank like a proverbial fish.

The elder brother aspired to be a zaddik, a righteous one, and to that end he applied himself with unmitigated diligence. Early in life he had been called by a deep inner longing to live an austere and ascetic existence. He prayed and studied ancient wisdom. He resisted comfort and complacency and avoided, as much as was humanly possible, all earthly pleasures. All, that is, except one. The sole diversion he did allow himself, if it could be called that, was to sing each evening a single hymn of jubilation.

The positive example set by the elder brother was, needless to say, not for a moment emulated by the younger. Quite to the contrary, the only mandates which the younger brother was interested in fulfilling were those of his untamed urges. Indeed, it was with deliberation equal to that of his older brother's piety and goodness that the younger brother engaged in all manner of pleasure. His reckless, wasteful pursuits had made him a local legend, and truly his reputation was well deserved. "Eat, drink and be merry!" might well have been his motto, although, "Live for today for tomorrow we may die!" would have applied just as aptly. For he could eat any three men under the table, and was sometimes heard to threaten that he might one day drink the entire county dry—a threat which was not lightly taken. He was the life of any party and quite a lady's man, too. The younger brother was always accompanied by a close circle of promiscuous women and a cluster of friends.

For fear that the reader might credit the younger brother's popularity to wit, charisma, charm, or even to his vainly handsome appearance, it should be explained that such was anything but the case. Nor should the younger brother's renowned generosity be mistaken as an emblem of a compassionate heart. In truth, the state of affairs that existed then was no different than the one that endures to this day. It has never been terribly difficult to find those who would gladly assist one in squandering an inheritance, no matter how meager it might happen to be. And as for the younger brother's generosity, it was born not from kindness, but rather from guilt, so deeply ingrained that it was not even perceived by him, much less admitted to. Unlike the elder brother who had been a good and dutiful son, the younger brother had rarely lifted so much as a finger in his late father's behalf.

Lest the reader be inundated by mistaken impressions, it must also be clarified, before this humble parable advances one sentence further, that the notable contrast in their personalities caused the brothers to harbor no great animosity toward each other. Despite their differences, there was, in fact, hardly a morsel of hostility between them. Their upbringing by a kindly merchant, recently deceased, and a loving, doting mother instilled in them tolerance and a disposition to live and let live. They got on well, for the most part, though neither approved of the other's way of life. They had their share of arguments, though in the end when the heat of the battle cooled, all would be forgiven.

It came as no great surprise when the two brothers bid farewell to their separate circles of friends, gave their mother farewell kisses and numerous assurances of their safe return, and set out walking one sunny morning in the late spring of the year 1653 toward a distant mecca of art, commerce and culture. Their intended aims and expectations for making this journey, like the brothers themselves, were as different as night and day. The elder brother hoped to find a certain zaddik who was rumored to be seeking a spiritual apprentice. The younger brother, however, had heard tales of the city's many lewd and passionate pleasures, of which he hoped to sample all but a few.

The days passed amicably. Mile after mile, village after village, county after county, they walked, conversing and arguing good-naturedly, occasionally pausing to gaze upon some uncommon sight, to hear some unusual sound, or to rest and eat by the banks of an algae-laden pond or a fast-running brook. At night they went their separate ways. While the elder brother read the Torah by firelight, meditated, and sang his nightly hymn, the younger brother would either eat and drink himself into a stupor or would go off in search of women and song. He had no need to search for wine, for he always made sure he carried a generous supply with him.

On their journey the younger brother was attacked by a band of thieves who sprang from the bushes, beat him about the head and shoulders, and made off with his purse. Luckily, this was one rare instance when the young reckless and wasteful brother had the uncustomary foresight to give the better part of his money to his brother for safekeeping. All he suffered on that occasion was a minor financial loss, a slightly blackened eye, and a mild case of wounded pride. Luck was also with him on another evening when a jealous husband, with a lantern jaw and hammer fists, tripped on a cobblestone, thus allowing him the precious seconds he needed to make a clean escape.

A week passed, and the better part of another. The halfway point was well behind them. The elder brother felt thoroughly invigorated. Not so the younger brother whose constant drunkenness and nightly jaunts were taking a heavy toll. Mornings were most difficult for him. He detested rising until the sun's disagreeable glare had begun to wane in the evening sky. On the road, however, it was imperative for them to put in as many miles as possible during daylight hours.

Rather than admit to the adverse effects of his over-indulgence, the younger brother would always bravely rise at the elder's prodding, laugh off his aching head and pretend that all was well. Thus, he would stoically go forth with throbbing temples and squinty, dark-rimmed, bloodshot eyes, a dull ache in the pit of his stomach, and a sour aftertaste left over from the previous evening's revelry that often would linger through most of the day.

As might be expected, the younger brother soon tired of this imposing appearance and was greatly pleased and relieved when a fierce storm struck one evening at a time when they happened to be in sight of a rustic, though agreeable looking, village inn which would, he hoped, afford him a quiet room, a hot bath, and a chance to recuperate from the past night's adventures. His expectations, however, proved ill-founded. When the two brothers inquired as to the availability of lodgings, the innkeeper, though seemingly sympathetic, informed them that several other travelers before them had sought shelter from the storm, the result being that every room was taken. After seeing the younger brother's debilitated condition, the innkeeper did offer, for a modest sum, to set up two cots in a corner of the room that was used by the inn's patrons for eating and drinking alcoholic beverages.

While in no sense an ideal situation, the brothers considered the cold, wet alternative and accepted the innkeeper's offer—the elder brother thinking that perhaps fate had brought him here with the object of furthering his spiritual education; the younger brother having no thoughts other than to rest his aching head and weary bones. While he was reluctant to admit it, the younger brother was feeling more flushed, feverish, and utterly wretched with every passing minute and wanted nothing more than to sink into oblivion.

Ruddy, rowdy, rotund, figures crammed the smoke-drenched dining room. Townsfolk, farmers, peasants, and travelers were talking, smoking, drinking, laughing and all of them seemingly intent upon making as much noise as possible while consuming as much as was humanly possible. These were the younger brother's kind of people, and on any other night he would have joined the festivities, but on this particular evening the very sight of so much gusto was enough to cause his head to spin and his stomach to do lazy cartwheels in sympathy.

While the innkeeper and his wife were setting up two cots in a shaded corner of the room, three of the patrons, thick of hand and girth, called over to the brothers in drink-thickened voices, offering to buy them a drink. The brothers smiled politely, waved across the noisy smoke-filled room while patting their lumpy hay-filled mattresses as if to say, "Thanks but no thanks," and the three burly men resumed their drinking.

At the younger brother's request, the elder brother took the cot nearest the wall, while the younger brother occupied the one closest to the night's festivities. The younger brother's location was based on the possibility that his dizzy head and churning stomach might give him cause to bring about a hasty retreat out of the thick, unpainted, weathered-hardwood door. Thus they settled in as best they could, to sleep.

The elder brother had not the least difficulty getting to sleep. Minutes later, when the younger brother complained about the smoke and the noise, the elder brother, who was facing the wall, snoozed heavily in reply. For the younger brother's sleep was as illusive as a swarm of fruit flies. The noise, the smoke, the uproar and laughter seemed in his increasingly feverish condition to be conspiring against him. The laughter and clatter seemed to be mocking him, twisting his ears, prying open his sweat glands, stirring up the vat of vinegar soup in his stomach while drilling pin-size holes in the sides of his head to release the resulting fumes. The evening's revelry seemed to be going on right inside his skull, his nerve endings, and in the very marrow of his bones. At other times, the babel of voices no longer seemed human, but like the barking of a kennel full of rabid strays. He tossed and twisted, stirring restlessly for an hour or two, before those yelping hounds of hell dragged him, kicking and screaming, into a fitful though blessed insensibility.

About that time it dawned upon the three thick-set revelers, who had earlier asked the brothers to share a drink with them, that perhaps the two strangers had refused them not out of simple fatigue, as their motions had seemed to suggest. Instead, perhaps, one of them suggested, their refusal to drink with them might have been the result of just plain "high-and-mightiness." Perhaps, added another, in the coarsest imaginable language, they thought themselves too good to drink with three men who made their living by the sweat of their brows and the strength of their backs. In no time, the brothers' simple gesture of refusal, in the hazy brains of the three muscle-bound drunkards, had been blown all out of proportion, taking on the dimensions of a hard slap across the face. Worse, an insult to their manhood! More serious even than that, a curse on their grandmothers' graves! This was exactly the sort of effrontery that no self-respecting oaf could, in good conscience, take sitting down.

With this in mind, the three ruddy-faced drunkards arose laboriously from their overburdened chairs and wobbled over to have a closer look at the two insolent snobs who had the foolishness and rash boldness to judge good men based upon the sketchiest evidence. Whereupon they loudly cursed and belittled the manhood of those who would spurn them and then rudely sleep through such a glorious festival of over-indulgence as they had offered to share with these two sleeping ingrates.

Being that the younger brother's cot was positioned nearest them, it was he upon whom the brutes started beating. A hand must have instinctively leapt out as he was waking and struck one of his attackers quite forcibly on the cheek. At least that was one of the complaints lodged against him as they hauled him from his bed, still half asleep, and commenced to push him around and then to slap him and hit him with repeated blows to his body and his undefended face and head.

As for the possibility of freeing himself, there was none. As for reasoning with them, that too was impossible. His protests fell on deaf ears. As for why they were doing this, he had not the slightest idea. All he did know was that three vaguely familiar brutes with hot, stale breath, scowling red-veined faces, and anvils where their hands should have been, were beating him half senseless for no apparent reason. Worse, his fever and depleted condition gave him neither the strength nor the conviction to give back even half so good as he was getting. So there he was, hardly able to defend himself and without even the benefit of his customary instinct for self-preservation, which under normal circumstances was quite considerable.

Fortunately for the sake of our young casualty, the innkeeper intervened to mediate on his behalf before the brutes had inflicted upon him serious injury. This act of intervention was hastily nullified by other deeds which were, to the victim's way of thinking, an outright travesty of justice. Instead of having the louts arrested, as the owner of any respectable establishment would have done, or at the very least escorting the drunkards to a bum's rush into the cold night, the innkeeper coddled the thugs and called them all by name! Instead of a swift kick into the stormy night, he gently chided the drunken brawlers in a tone that carried no more indignity than one would use on an errant child who had purposefully spilled a glass of milk. Was this not an outrage? Here he was, simply ushering the ruffians back to their table, leaving the battered victim with nothing but an apology for what was euphemistically termed "an inconvenience!"

Contempt gave way to bitterness, pain to self-pity, as the younger brother sat on the lumpy mattress and nursed his wounds. He had a split lip, a lump on his head, possibly a cracked rib or worse, and his attackers were back at their seats ordering another round and being treated as if they had created no more than a minor annoyance. Where was the fairness in this world? Where was the justice?

And where had his brother been while all this was going on? Hard though it was to imagine, the man had been, and still was, deep in slumber! Dead to the world! Sleeping like a statue! Why does one not travel alone, he angrily wondered, if not for sake of having one's traveling companions there for protection? A wave of incoherence suddenly came crashing over the rocky shore of his inner being, causing him to conclude, unreasonably, that somehow his sleeping brother was to blame. Whereupon, he leaned over and roughly shook the elder brother.

The elder brother awoke to a barrage of harsh criticism for not having risen to his brother's defense. Seeing his brother's condition, he felt only sympathy for him and not the slightest contempt. Indeed, his compassion grew more emphatic with his relating of each passing affront and insult. The poor man had obviously reached his breaking point. Finally, with quiet words of comfort, he persuaded his younger brother to try to go back to sleep. The younger brother agreed to this suggestion in principle, but fearing a repeat performance by the brutes, asked that the elder switch beds with him. The elder brother more then gladly complied, as any loving brother would have done under similar circumstances.

Be not mistaken as to the nature of the motivations of those who aspire to become zaddikim. While it may be true that a zaddik does not shy away from life's hardships and uncertainties, and it is true that he denies bodily comfort, he does so not out of some masochistic yearning, but for the purpose of achieving the greater pleasure that can be derived by completing the soul's cycle of correction. Thus the elder brother welcomed the opportunity to place himself between the thugs and his irate brother. If his body did receive a beating, well so be it! Certainly it would be for a reason. Perhaps some wrong deed in the past demanded retribution. At all events, he would accept what fate or providence had in store, firm in the conviction that the pain suffered by his body would be serving a higher purpose, namely, the purification of his soul. And so it was that the two brothers traded places and eventually drifted off to sleep.

Sure enough, later in the evening, as fate would have it, or perhaps it was providence, it dawned upon one of the three thugs that they had attacked only one of the disrespectful strangers, while sparing the other. This, in his inebriated judgment, did not seem equitable. Both were guilty of the same holier-than-thou impudence. Both had demonstrated equal conceit by refusing to share a drink with them. In good conscience, they could not beat up on only one of the contemptuous newcomers and let the other off scot free. Justice demanded that the other receive equal retribution. The incident, long forgotten by the brothers but in the benumbed brains of the three brutes, had become a matter of honor, principle, and integrity. Fair, after all, was only fair.

The brutes rose from their seats and lumbered over to the shadowed corner in which the two brothers were sleeping, both of them facing the wall. The thugs had no idea that the two brothers had switched beds, so quite naturally it was the man who was sleeping in the bed closest to the wall who was the target of their animosity. Thinking that the man closest to them had already received his comeuppance, they took great pains not to disturb him. They dragged the younger brother out of bed a second time and gave him a thorough beating, while the elder slept like a newborn babe.

A strange sensation overcame the younger brother as his body was suffering that second attack. Attribute it to fever, a concussion, or merely the utter absurdity of the situation, but he hardly felt the blows that were hailing upon him from all sides and angles. Whatever the cause, he was suddenly catapulted into an exquisite state of awareness, higher, purer, more lucid by far than any he had previously imagined. In those moments of mystical recognition his life came into clear and perfect focus. The facade of illusion with which he had always protected himself began to crack and then to crumble, leaving him alone with the naked reality of his empty existence. He saw it all: the futility of his self-indulgence and pursuit of pleasure, the vulgarity of his coarse nature and the true agony of his moral decay.

Those few seconds of mystical revelation taught him more than a lifetime of self-indulgence. And to whom did he owe this transformation, if not the brutes? He laughed! How he laughed! Which, as it happened, did much toward lessening the severity of the beating. So uproarious did his laughter become that the oafs lost the thread of their concentration and became confused and disoriented. Little satisfaction can be derived, especially from one who takes pleasure in the beating!

The elder brother awoke to the sound of laughter, not just that of his brother but of others that had also been bitten by the contagious laughter, including the brutes themselves! At that moment, he too underwent something of a transformation, for he understood what had happened and immediately realized that indeed fate, or some power higher than themselves, had guided them to this inn on this rain-swept night.

The two brothers never did complete their journey to the city. They had no need to. In that one evening they had intuitively transcended any further need for restless wandering and the emotional agonies that pass for worldly experiences. And so it was that they returned to their village. The two brothers had become "zaddikim" or righteous ones. They lived long, productive, loving lives in the village and through the years many seekers traveled from far and wide to request their counsel or simply to pay respects.

In their later years, the two wise zaddikim would sometimes recall with fondness the night in the village inn, and remember the two beatings which the younger had suffered at the hands of those three brutes. And, as always, they would smile, bless the brutes, and thank them in their evening prayers.

All opposites reflect the conciliating principle itself, namely the Tao. Yin and Yang. Right and Wrong. Good and Evil. The Tao mirrors the complementary aspects of one and the same reality. Opposites are inseparable and arise simultaneously and mutually—just two different names for one process. The truth contains many contradictions, creating two worlds from aspects of one underlying reality which transcends and encompasses them both.

> They said to Him: Shall we then being children, enter the kingdom? Jesus said to them: When you make the two one, the outer as the inner, and the above as the below, and when you make the male and the female into a single one then you shall enter the kingdom.

Gospel of St. Thomas

All that exists in the sphere of thought in the manifestations of time and space will pass. Life will be no more. The things that you personally have long forgotten or can easily forget are happening to you now, and will happen to you again tomorrow. The endless toils and pleasures of everyday existence will be forgotten.

> A powerful king, ruler of many domains, was in a position of such magnificence that wise men were his mere employees. And yet one day he felt himself confused and called his sages to him.
>
> He said: "I do not know the cause, but something impels me to seek a certain ring, one that will enable me to stabilize my state. I must have such a ring, and this ring must be one which, when I am unhappy it will make me joyful and at the same time, if I am happy and look upon it I must be made sad."
>
> The wise men consulted one another, and threw themselves into deep contemplation. Finally they came to a decision as to the character of this ring which would suit their king.
>
> The ring which they devised was one upon which was inscribed the legend:

"THIS, TOO, WILL PASS"

All happenings in our finite existence within time and space will ultimately come to an end. At that time our life will seem to have been senseless and useless. Or will it? This is the paradox.

The angel of death came to a lost soul one evening and said, "It is time for you to come with me." "I am not ready," he said. "I have a lot of work yet to accomplish. I must do this and that and be here and there." "You still must come," said the angel of death.

"Take my son instead of me," said this lost and wretched soul. The angel of death was surprised by such a request and said, "You are not serious are you?" "Yes, I am," said the lost and wretched soul, "Take my son."

"I have never had a request such as this before," said the angel of death. He turned and asked the son, "Are you willing to go in your father's place?" and the son replied, "I love my father with all of my heart and I am willing to go in his place." The angel of death accepted the trade and left.

After another lifetime the angel of death came back and said, "It is now time to go." And this lost soul again said, "No! I am not ready to go, I have so much more to do, you must take my other son." And again the angel of death was surprised and asked the son, "Would you like to go in your father's place?" The son said, "I love my father with all of my heart and soul and I will go in his place."

Another hundred years passed and another. Each time the angel of death came for this lost soul, and left with another one of his sons. After a thousand years passed, the angel of death came again to take another son and the father said, "No! this time you will not take any more of my sons. It is time for me to go."

This surprised the angel of death and he asked, "What has changed?" The enlightened soul with grace and love replied, "After all these years, I have seen my sons go in my place because of their love for me. I did not realize that they had found the meaning and purpose of life at such a young age. It has taken me a thousand years to become aware that love is the only meaning and purpose of life. No matter how long I live, my work will never be finished and nothing is more important than love."

Greater love has no one than this that one lay down his life for his friends.

John 15:13

"Vanity of vanities," says the Preacher, "Vanity of vanities! All is vanity." What advantage does man have in all his work which he does under the sun? A generation goes and a generation comes, but the earth remains forever. Also, the sun rises and the sun sets; And hastening to its place it rises there again. Blowing toward the south, then turning toward the north, the wind continues swirling along and on its circular courses the wind returns.

All the rivers flow into the sea, yet the sea is not full. To the place from which the rivers flow, there they flow again. All things are wearisome; Man is not able to tell it. The eye is not satisfied with seeing, nor is the ear filled with hearing. That which has been is that which will be, and that which has been done is that which will be done.

So, there is nothing new under the sun. Is there anything of which one might say, "See this, it is new"? Already it has existed for ages which were before us. There is no remembrance of earlier things; And also of the later things which will occur. There will be for them no remembrance among those who will come later still.

Ecclesiastes 1:2-11

The conclusion, when all has been heard, is: fear God and keep His commandments, because this applies to every person. For God will bring every act to judgment, everything which is hidden, whether it is good or evil.

Ecclesiastes 12:13-14

Lord, make me know the measure of my days on earth, to consider my frailty that I must perish. Surely, all my days here are as a handbreadth to Thee, and my lifetime is as naught to Thee. Verily, mankind walketh in a vain show, and their best state is vanity. Man passeth away like a shadow, he is disquieted in vain, he heapeth up riches, and cannot tell who shall gather them. Now Lord, what do I wait for? My hope is in Thee.

God's presence, love, and wisdom are a state of consciousness that enables one to transcend the objects of one's desires that lie within the finite conditions of opposites in the realm of time and space, to the realization of the glory, beauty, and majesty of His essential Being.

LIFE

Life is but time and space
And means nothing until it's placed
Into the hearts of those we love
Which is cherished like a dove.

Ruth E Rapanos

Man's distinctions between good and evil have no meaning for God, who knows only unity. Your attitude towards everything in this world must be one of detachment, for if one does not equate the good of this world with its evil, he is not unifying himself with his source completely. To the Spirit, no evil exists. Evil is but an illusion of life. God has allowed Evil solely to furnish man with the means of exercising his free will.

We are driven mercilessly like a helpless puppet, with the forces of nature and the environment apparently pulling the strings. The world is indifferent and its everyday events are like a puppeteer pulling the strings of a marionette jester in an attempt to expose the face of glory.

> The forms which clothe existence only stay
> One moment, in the next they pass away;
> This subtle point is proven by the text,
> Its fashion altereth from one day to the next.[1]

Life in its transitory nature is senseless and useless but if suffering is the means for transformation, then life has served its purpose and is not senseless and useless after all.

In this relative world, in this wondrous structure of the universe, everything is interrelated and interdependent. This great universe would not respond to a warm and glowing celebration of sympathy and love if it were not for the conscious awareness of good and evil, happiness and sorrow in the memories of men.

> I live with evil while my self is here;
> With God both self and evil disappear.[1]

For the spirit there is neither death nor evil. Death and evil are for the flesh, but not for the spirit. The way of paradoxes is the way of Truth, ordained by the ever essence of our existence; so one could experience His presence. Beyond life's paradoxes, one sees God against the clear mirror of his own soul.

Die Before You Die

I must die, but when? I will meet God, but how? I will live in eternity, but where?

If you die before you die, then when you die, you will not die. An interesting paradox. No one becomes as aware of God as the one who is throughly dead. There is but one immortal Self common in and to us all—that which remains untouched by the flight of time.

> The heavens and all the works of His hand proclaim God's glory.
>
> Psalm 19:1

Astrologers can help you understand
With fine configurations traced in sand—
You've seen one draw the heaven's calendar
And indicate each fixed and moving star,
Set out the zodiac sign by mighty sign,
The zenith of the sun and its decline—
The complex forms that influence the earth,
The house of mournful death, the house of birth,
Which will enable him to calculate
Your happiness, your grief, your final fate. . .
Then brush the sand—and all that you have seen
Has gone, as though the marks had never been.
Such is the solid world we live in here,
A subtle surface which will disappear.[1]

All that lives must die, passing through nature to eternity. One must realize that he is going to die. His body is going to decay. Although there is another kind of death, a voluntary death, not a natural death, not that of the body, but that of the mind. The ego, the mind, must die and be resurrected, not as "I" but as "Thou."

As long as you do not know
How to die and come to life again,
You are but a sorry traveler,
On this dark earth.

Goethe

If you put all your trust in "I" and "me"
You've chosen both worlds as your enemy—
But if you kill the self, the darkest night
Will be illuminated with your light.[1]

Dying before you die is dying to your separate-self (ego). The seed dies in order to experience itself as a tree or flower. Man must die to his separate-self in order to experience his true Self in God. In essence the seed does not die, it evolves. Man does not die, he unfolds.

While the seed lacks nothing, it is only the fruit
that realizes that the seed lacks nothing.

The breakthrough comes when the ego, the craving and desires of the mind, are overcome. He that overcometh fear shall not be in fear of the second death. Fear is the mother of all evil.

There is no fear in love; but perfect love casteth out fear.

1 John 4:18

To him that overcometh I will give him eternal life that no man knoweth saving he that receiveth it.

Man has received from heaven a soul, a nature innately good, to guide him in all his movements. By devotion to this divine spirit within himself, he attains the pure innocence that leads him to do right with instinctive sureness, and without any ulterior thought of reward and personal advantage.

If you die to the ego—the separate-self, the mind, to all that was human—you become available to the infinite sources of existence. This breakthrough will appear to you like a death, because your present finite identity will be lost.

> Who knoweth if to die
> Be but to live
> And that called life by mortals
> Be but death.

> Euripides

When your present finite identity is lost, that which was always hidden within you but unrealized will come forth in all its splendrous glory.

> Glorification means deification, resurrection and transformation. Resurrection and transformation to glorification and deification.

You will become aware that what existed in the past was like a dream, an illusion; and what is real is the resurrection of the present moment in God-consciousness—a rebirth to a nonconditional mode of Being where things decayed and loved ones lost in dreamy shadows rise. The birth that occurs is a Self-awakening. The soul is born again in God.

Resurrection is possible only when you are capable of dying to the consciousness of the ego (the human condition) and being in union with God. Complete silence mirrors the existence of God. In that moment within the silence of one's soul everything is achieved. You realize your nature perfectly.

> It is the face you had the day before your great-grandfather was born.

You do not identify with your separate-self, but with the whole world. Everything becomes you. This would be the death of the ego (separate-self) experience. Your true Self is now the whole world.

> I am not I because I am egoless, and yet I am absolutely I because I am my true Self. Likewise, you are not you because you are egoless, and yet you are absolutely you because you are your true Self. Moreover, since I am not I, I am you, and since you are not you, you are I.

Your body will die; your mind will die; your ego will die; all that can die will die. Only the essence of your conscious being will remain. Die as you are, so that you can become that which you really are. Die to the ego, so that the Divine can be born in you. Die to the past, so you can be open to the present. Die to the future, so you can live in the present. Die to the mind, so the love of God can be rediscovered in your heart. Die to the known, so the unknown can penetrate in you. It is an awareness of the soul that was separated from the love of God, because of the boundaries the mind had created.

But until you die to the ego, you live a deathless death. A life in death.

> Her lips were red, her looks were free,
> Her locks were yellow as gold:
> Her skin was as white as leprosy,
> The Night-mare Life-in-Death was she.[2]

> Yet lay the weight so close about
> There was no room for it without.
> And so beneath the weight lay I
> And suffered death, but could not die.[3]

That which separates us from our God-given nature must be lost before we are able to become aware of our true nature. The only way to gain it is to lose it.

> For whoever wants to save his life will lose it
> but whoever loses his life for my sake will find
> it.

Matthew 16:25

Life is paradoxical. Surrender takes a great will and when you surrender you will lose yourself. Your absence becomes His presence. You become Self aware. He comes with Grace only when you are empty, like a lit candle that kisses an unlit candle and departs.

> You cannot hope for Life till you progress.
> Through some small shadow of this Nothingness.
> First He will humble you in dust and mire,
> And then bestow the glory you desire.
> Be nothing first! and then you will exist,
> You cannot live whilst life and self persist—
> Till you reach Nothingness you cannot see
> The Life you long for in eternity.[1]

Both subject and object must be denied, and one must transform the perceptions of duality into a nondualistic mode. He must forget himself and become aware that he is one with the process—the essence of life itself—and, in changing, he will be at rest.

> Stop Christian passer-by!—Stop, child of God,
> And read with gentle breast. Beneath this sod
> A poet lies, or that which once seem'd he.
> O lift one thought in prayer for S. T. C.;
> That he who many a year with toil of breath
> Found death in life, may here find life in death!
> Mercy for praise—to be forgiven for fame
> He ask'd, and hoped, through Christ.
> Do thou the same!

Epitaph of Samuel Taylor Coleridge

Until you die to the ego (the person you identify with) you will never know who you truly are. The supreme sacrifice is not only of the human condition, but also of the personality. Man must die to this life and sacrifice the personality that has evolved from the human condition. When your ego, your separate-self dies, you experience what Jesus calls life abundant. You overflow with it.

> In order to arrive at being everything, desire to be nothing.
>
> Saint John of the Cross

Empty oneself.   Buddhism

To learn the Buddhist Way is to learn about oneself and to forget oneself to the extent that one becomes aware of a consciousness pervading everywhere and everything. To forget oneself is to perceive oneself as all things. To realize this is to cast off the body and mind of self and others. Transcending the body and mind man is eternally one with the infinite—one's own true Self.

> If a man empties himself of himself, who can harm him?
>
> Chuang-tse

Does enlightenment involve becoming empty, or expanding to encompass everything? To become empty is to become everything; and to experience everything as One is again equivalent to being empty, although a different sense of emptiness. Is the drop poured into the ocean, or is the ocean poured into the drop? An interesting paradox for those who see.

To experience the Truth, the Absolute, it is necessary to empty yourself, to "let go" completely, in order to realize that consciousness is nothing other than "me" fully becoming what I have always been—a conscious awareness of "Being." The person behind the mask. The truth beneath the disguise. The light beyond the shadow.

The breakthrough comes when the ego dies and the soul and the body are united in harmony with the laws of the natural order of the universe. When this happens one will not fear the natural death of the body. The body may come to an end, but consciousness does not.

Benjamin Franklin's Epitaph

The Body of B. Franklin, Printer,
Like the cover of an old book,
Its contents worn out,
And stript of its lettering and gilding
Lies here, Food for worms.
But the work shall not be lost;
For it will, as he believed, appear once more
In a new and more elegant Edition
Corrected and improved
By the Author.

Benjamin Franklin

Nature has engraved her own image and that of her Author on all things.

Through the death of the ego, immortality is achieved. Your authentic being will burst forth in all its glory. It was before you were born, it is here in the present moment, and it will be there after you die.

Everything is possible when the mind becomes the humble servant of God and not its master. Your mind must accept, surrender, and totally submit to the will of God.

Seek ye first the Kingdom of God and all its righteousness; and all things shall be added unto you.

Matthew 6:33

Love—Virtue

Love is the physician of the Universe. Love invites the soul to return home to the fields of Divine Glory.

Every man is ultimately destined to move from the human to the supernatural dimension of experience. One should not be obsessed with a passing love. One should be in love with the beloved and the beloved is God. A rose is a rose, but in its transcendental form it is the image and shadow of God. A rose is a rose is a rose. . . . . A rose by any other name is still a rose.

Furnace of love's fire, yet it is the rose garden of the soul.

Is it not delightful to be in love? It does not last, because it does not belong to the earth; and when you clasp the idol it turns out to be a rag doll. For the immortal part must elude you if you grab at it.

George Bernard Shaw

First burn the self, and as its fate is sealed
The gems this idol hides will be revealed.[1]

Divine beauty is revealed in human beauty. One must pass beyond shadows to Reality. The beloved in your heart is the living experience and Self-awareness of the Divine within you. Ordinary human love is capable of raising man to the experience of real love. Love becomes perfect only when it transcends itself and becomes One with its object, producing a Unity of Being.

Life is a series of lessons to see things purely as objects of love; true love, peace, and fulfillment lie beyond the object of one's desires. Fulfillment then becomes not a matter of self-indulgence, but of Self-awareness.

And as she glimpsed his face she felt her heart,
Her intellect, her self-control depart—
Now reason fled and love usurped its reign;
Her sweet soul trembled in love's bitter pain.[1]

Do you not know that you are everything to me? But I myself do not know what peace of mind means, nor can I give it to you. I can give you my whole being, my whole love; yes, but I cannot separate you from myself in my own thoughts. To my eyes you and I are one. I can see one of two things—only despair or happiness—and what happiness!

Anna Karenine-Leo Tolstoi

The faithful lover enjoys the tribulations sent by his beloved. In default of happiness, there is a bittersweet pleasure in suffering through what we love.

How savage is love
    that plants a flower
    and uproots a field
that revives us
    for a day
      and stuns us
          for an age!

*

How peaceful life would be without love. How safe, how tranquil and how dull.

The Name of the Rose

The object of one's love is the form through which one contemplates a radiant source of light, which is divine beauty. She is contemplated as essence, no longer veiled, for it is through her that the face of God is seen. She is the eternal goddess who is hidden within the self. A woman for whom your soul you would give.

> To the celestial and my soul's idol, the most beautiful Ophelia.[4]

> Doubt that the stars are on fire,
> Doubt that the sun does shine,
> Doubt truth to be a liar,
> But never doubt this love of mine.

The greatest pain that leads to salvation is to see your love suffer. Love always suffers with its beloved. Love moves the soul to contrition, where love unites the soul to God and brings us to Heaven.

> A lighter sin or a lesser error
> Might change through hope or fear divine;
> But there is no fear and hell has no terror,
> To change or alter a love like mine.[13]

> I crowned her with bliss,
>   and she me with thorn;
> I brought her to worship,
>   and she me to scorn;

> Her hate made never,
>   my love her foe;
> She fled, I followed,
>   I loved her so.

> Should the happiness I have dared to dream of come to me, it would be beyond mere human happiness.

You will never truly experience God and find peace—the pearl of great worth—by way of a passing love until you purge yourself of this love and stop mistaking the object of your love for the prize. The prize being the hidden treasure that lies deep within your soul.

Ah! Love, could you and I with fate conspire
To mend this sorry scheme of things entire,
Would we not shatter it to bits, and then
Remould it nearer to the heart's desire?

Omar Khayyam

The object of your love only leads you to the inner depths of your Being where you will come to realize and experience the Source of your existence—the Source from whom all blessings flow.

The love of the object was man's journey "to" God. The process and act of love is man's journey "into" God. The source of true love lies beyond the object of attention.

Love for the young and peace for the old is basically a matter of perception. Love for the young is a love for the object. Peace for the old is a love that transcends the object and attains fulfillment within the heart and love of God. Different objects do not alter true love's passion.

Many a man has loved you with love false and true. But only one man has loved the virgin soul in you.

George Rapanos

"How shall I find the words for the beauty of my Beloved? For He is merged in all beauty," says Kabir. "His color is in all pictures of the world." Beauty is simply Reality seen with the eyes of love.

I saw perfection's image, beauty's queen,
A vision that no man has ever seen.
If on its path love forces you to yield,
Then do so gladly, throw away your shield.
True lovers give up everything they own
To steal one moment with the Friend alone.[1]

Let me not to the marriage of true minds
Admit impediments; love is not love
Which alters when it alteration finds
Or bends with the remover to remove.
Oh, no, it is an ever-fixed mark
That looks on tempest and is never shaken;
It is the star to every wand'ring bark,
Whose worth's unknown, although his height be taken.
Love's not Time's fool, though rosy lips and cheeks
Within his bending sickle's compass come;
Love alters not with his brief hours and weeks,
But bears it out even to the edge of doom.
    If this be error, and upon me proved,
    I never writ, nor no man ever loved.[4]

Love which does not care to bend to love's requests is empty air. The fruit of the Spirit is love, joy, peace, patience, kindness, generosity, faithfulness, gentleness, and self-control. By acquiring the attributes of God, man becomes one with virtue. Out of the nature of virtue comes true love. The eternal core of Truth is love. True virtue consists of benevolence to being and is exercised in the general goodwill towards men.

Life is an enchantress
Who seduces us with her beauty
But he who knows (discerns) her beauty
Will transcend her enchantments.

Life is an enchantress
Who seduces us with her beauty
But he who knows (discerns) her wiles
Will flee her enchantments.

The great goddess, a maddening enchantress, is yet a bringer of wisdom—a voluptuous harlot and inviolable virgin, immemorially old and eternally young.

For she is also the goddess who fascinates and bewitches, the seducer and bringer of delight. The sovereign enchantress, who confuses the senses and drives men out of their minds. The sorceress who transforms men into animals.

> When I was one and twenty,
> I heard a wise man say,
> "Give crowns, pounds, and guineas,
> but not your heart away;
>
> Give rubies away and pearls,
> But keep your fancy free."
> For I was one and twenty,
> No use to talk to me.
>
> When I was one and twenty,
> I heard him say again,
> "The heart out of the bosom,
> Was never given in vain;
>
> Tis paid with sighs aplenty,
> And sold for endless rue."
> And now I'm two and twenty,
> Oh, "Tis true, tis true."

She remains eternally unfaithful to him and brings him nothing but misfortune. It is the curse and gift of mankind that these polar opposites, attraction-repulsion, love-hate, joy-sorrow, pleasure-pain, good-evil, yes and no should be continuously struggling for a life beyond death, where death is not the predestined end, and the mortality of the individual is not the only aspect of life. Nor is his dominion limited to this world alone, but on him depends the perfection of the higher worlds and of God himself.

There was something formless yet complete,
That existed before heaven and earth;
Without sound, without substance,
Dependent on nothing, unchanging,
All pervading, unfailing.
One may think of it as the mother of all things
in heaven.

Lao-tzu

Divine love is the mother of all good. The earth is the mother of us all. Man and earth are of one mind, the Self-subsisting life of the universe.

Man's life is the gift of nature, but beautiful living is a gift of wisdom. Our life is essentially a spiritual pilgrimage towards Divine fulfillment.

I will go a thousand leagues in falsehood, that
one step of the journey may be true.

Sufism

Wisdom profits from the years by drawing more fully on the Divine capacity which lives in every man.

Wisdom is glorious and never fadeth away.
Yes, she is easily seen of them that love her and
found of such as seek her.

Wisdom of Solomon 6:12

A being possessed by virtue experiences a grace in all that exists and is one in God. Only through love can we know that we are one with God. God is the experience of love, and he who loves is united with God.

Jesus said, "My Father is greater than I," and "The Father and I are one." In our finite self-consciousness, "My Father is greater than I." In infinite consciousness, "The Father and I are One." God is "Being," and from the spirit of His Being radiates love and compassion that encompasses all.

Doctor Truth

George went to Doctor Truth and told him that he was suffering. His hands were always taking things that did not belong to him. Doctor Truth said "It is your heart." George proceeded to tell Doctor Truth that his heart was fine and that he had other problems. His eyes were also causing him trouble. They were always lusting for the forbidden fruits. Doctor Truth said again, "It is your heart." George stormed out of the doctor's office shouting, "It is not my heart! I have never had a problem with my heart! My heart is fine!"

George then began to look for another doctor that could help him. As he went down the street, he saw a sign that read, DOCTOR BE GOOD. George went in. Doctor Be Good told George all that he had to do was to be good and all his problems would go away. George was as good as good could be, but now the problems festered inside of him, and would not go away.

He went searching for another doctor and it led him to Doctor Do Good. Doctor Do Good told him all he had to do was to do good and all his problems would be solved. Well, George did good. Whenever he saw an opportunity to do good, he was there. Yet his problems persisted.

George walked the streets in despair searching for another doctor and he came upon another sign that read DOCTOR RELIGION. This must be the answer, he said, and went in. Doctor Religion told him all he had to do to find the peace he was seeking was to go to church. George then faithfully went to church, but to no avail. The problems still persisted, so George went back to Doctor Religion for further instructions.

Doctor Religion asked him if he had joined the church. "Was I suppose to?" was George's reply. "Yes, by all means," said Doctor Religion. With new hope, George joined the church and was accepted by the total congregation. For awhile George felt good. Then the problems reappeared and he went back to Doctor Religion. He told him that he had joined the church and that he was accepted by the total congregation and for a period of time felt good. As time passed, George realized that whatever he did that he was told to do did not solve his problems and asked for further instructions.

Doctor Religion wanted to know if he had volunteered for any church functions. George said "No, was I suppose to?" "Why, yes, my son," was his reply. Then George volunteered. He volunteered for the choir. He volunteered to teach Sunday school. He volunteered whenever the need arose. It came to pass that during a Sunday sermon the preacher expounded on George's service to the church and the community. He said that, "Everyone should be like brother George." Yet this did not bring George the promised peace that he sought.

He left the church seeking another doctor when Doctor Truth appeared. "Did you find the peace you were searching for?" asked Doctor Truth. "No!" said George. "It is your heart, for it is heavy-laden," replied Doctor Truth. "I have tried everything and nothing has helped. What should I do?" asked George.

"Put your faith in me and everything will be all right. We must operate," he said. In despair George agreed and surrendered his will to Doctor Truth. When George awakened, after the operation, he felt fine. For the first time in his life he radiated love and compassion and was at peace with himself.

"I feel great," he said, "I have never felt better in my life. What did you do?" Doctor Truth replied, "We gave you a new heart." In bewilderment George said, "It is very difficult to believe and hard to understand. I thought my heart was in great shape all these years. Could it be that I was deceiving myself? Who's heart did you give me?" Doctor Truth answered, "The heart of Jesus."

> Jesus then went into the temple and drove out all those who were selling and buying there.

The true and living temple and sanctuary of God is the whole world of men united in love. When Jesus cast the money-changers out of the Temple, it represented the casting of the bargaining thoughts out of His body Temple. The bargaining motives of buying and selling the soul by being good and doing good to gain virtue, rather than virtue being the means of being and doing good. He who does good, without the strength of faith in his heart, knows neither duty nor virtue and thereby loses his reward.

> By their fruits ye shall know them.

Martyrdom often is used to camouflage cowardice. Martyrs can hide behind this mask of being good and unselfish as a way to avoid taking their journeys, and finding out the motives of their actions and who they really are.

These money-changers in the temple are like martyrs who are buying and selling favors to gain the kingdom of Heaven. The Temple is the soul. God wishes for it to be empty, so he can fill it with true virtue.

A Japanese master received a university professor who came to inquire about Zen.

The master served tea. He poured his visitor's cup full, and then kept on pouring.

The professor watched the overflow until he no longer could restrain himself. "It is overfull. No more will go in!"

"Like this cup," the master said, "you are full of your own opinions and speculations. How can I show you Zen unless you first empty your cup?"

If your cup is full, then how can anything of value enter? Life must be motivated by the essence of virtue.

You spoke of a curse that you could not escape. But there is something stronger than that. Love. And you must learn what it means. When you have learned that it means giving without any hope of return, that it means creating faith and belief in another; then you will know the true meaning of love. And the young man will say to you, "You are beautiful and your face is as beautiful as you are." Wear it and you will know the Truth.

> Giving isn't giving,
> Though the gift be tied,
> With ribbons, bows of gladness,
> What good the gift inside.

You give but little when you give of your possessions. It is when you give of yourself that you truly give.

There are those who give with joy, and that joy is their reward.

And there are those who give with pain, and that pain is their baptism.

And there are those who give and know not pain in giving, nor do they seek joy, nor give with mindfulness of virtue;

They give as in yonder valley the myrtle breathes its fragrance into space.

Through the hands of such as these God speaks, and from behind their eyes He smiles upon the earth.

Kahlil Gibran

Giving does not act from the love of rewards or the fear of punishment but rather from divine grace. We do not find joy in virtue because we control our lust, but because we find joy in virtue, we are able to control our lust.

Perfect kindness acts without thinking of kindness.

Virtue is its own reward, and vice its appropriate punishment. Our virtue and goodness are due to a higher state of consciousness and our weakness and blindness are due to our lower states of consciousness.

Superior virtue is not conscious of itself as virtue, and so really is virtue. Inferior virtue cannot let go of being virtuous and so is not virtue. Superior virtue does not seem to be busy and yet there is nothing which it does not accomplish. Inferior virtue is always busy and yet in the end leaves things undone.

Lao-tse

201

One must remove the darkness (ignorance) of who he really is by the light of knowledge and wisdom of the Masters to gain what is always there and surrender to Him.

> Virtue is a blessedness unto itself and an expression of God's presence in this world.

God is not a symbol of power over man, but of man's own power. Our attributes and those of God must be united in every way. When we realize that we possess the identical attributes of God, who is to say we are not God? Thus is God incarnate.

> But he who unites himself with the Lord is one with him in spirit.
>
> 1 Corinthians 6:17

Once your heart and soul become aware of the reality of the living God, your soul becomes fused with the attributes of God, and your motives and actions become one and the same with those of God.

Thou art a servant of God! Thou art an expression of God! Thou art a reflection of God! Thou art a co-worker with God! Look within! He is dwelling within you! A Hidden Treasure within the world of "Becoming."

> I was a hidden treasure and I desired to be known; therefore I created the creation in order that I might be known.
>
> I AM this whole world yet to be realized. Once realized I AM entangled through time and space. I and the universe are "One." I am no longer I AM THAT I AM. Instead I AM that which I perceive I am.

A man from a small Indian village once went to the market town to buy five donkeys. Since his village was quite far, he decided to ride back on the sturdiest of the donkeys, letting the others trail along. When he neared his home he wanted to make sure that all the five donkeys were still with him. He looked back and counted, and discovered that there were only four donkeys. He cursed himself for not paying closer attention to them during the journey, and arrived home in a dejected mood. As he was getting off the donkey he told his wife, who had come out to greet him. "I feel very sad. I bought five donkeys, but somehow I lost one on the way." The wife looked at him and remarked, "you are right, there are not five donkeys,—there are six!"

Similarly, a thing may be with you, but if you do not recognize it, you effectively disown it and go about searching for it. Such a search is an illegitimate one, to be solved only by knowing that the thing is, in fact, with you all the time.

THE HIDDEN TREASURE
"The Pearl of Great Worth"

There is a hidden Treasure,
Most search for it in vain.
It comes down from heaven,
And it falls like the rain.

This treasure is not one of silver,
This treasure is not one of gold.
The source of this hidden treasure,
Lies deep within one's soul.

A treasure more precious than silver,
A treasure more precious than gold.
To find this hidden treasure,
You must look within your soul.[9]

The basis of every man's existence is to live in harmony with God and bring together the values of the cosmic-universal conscious mind within the experiences of everyday living.

It is a life fully integrated with the life force of the universe, finding fulfillment in the surrender of everyday desires to the will of the divine presence within the world of multiplicity. Man's life is to be a bridge between the divine life and the whole of creation, acting with absolute freedom to the spontaneity of the moment.

> Live in the universal consciousness to know no self but that which is reflected, not only from within your heart and soul but from the faces of those all around you—from your fellow creatures, the flowers, the trees, the beasts, yea from the very surface of the water and the sands of the desert.

God in himself is infinite love. Love is the spiritual expression of God in which we all have our beginning. Love is a divine visitation. Only through love will we experience God.

This experience of Self-love will liberate you from the confusions that the trials and tribulations present in life, which hold you in bondage and cause you to suffer.

The Koran is the revealed scripture of Islam, transmitted to Mohammed by Gabriel between Allah and His messenger.

Selfishness

Selfishness causes suffering and is not identical with Self-love, but with its very opposite. Self-love is the love of God for all mankind, expressing itself within and through you. Selfishness is self-love, which excludes love of others—a kind of greediness. Like all greediness, it contains an insatiability, as a consequence of which there is never any real satisfaction. Greed is a bottomless pit which exhausts the person in an endless effort to satisfy the need without ever reaching satisfaction.

> How much land do you want? Not much; only
> the land that touches mine.

Close observation shows that while the selfish person is always anxiously concerned with himself, he is never satisfied, is always restless, driven by the fear of not getting enough, of missing something, of being deprived of something. He is filled with burning envy of anyone who might have more.

> Their prayers know nothing of love's selfless pain;
> Not love inspires them but mere lust for gain.[1]

If we observe still closer, especially the unconscious dynamics, we find that this type of person is basically not fond of himself, but deeply dislikes himself.

Selfishness is essentially conservative and hates being disturbed. It prefers an easygoing, unexacting lie to the greatest truth, if the latter requires the sacrifice of one's smallest comfort.

Selfishness is rooted in the very lack of fondness for one's self. The person who is not fond of himself, who does not approve of himself, is in constant anxiety concerning his own self. He has not the inner security which can exist only on the basis of genuine fondness and affirmation. He is only concerned about himself, greedy to get everything for himself, since basically he lacks security and satisfaction.

The same holds true with the so-called narcissistic person, who is not so much concerned with getting things for himself as with admiring himself. He is in love with the beauty of his own reflection. While on the surface it seems that these people are very much in love with themselves, they actually are not fond of themselves. It is an overcompensation for the basic lack of Self-love. Unless you can love and trust yourself, you cannot love or trust others. A narcissistic person is forever suffering, because he has withdrawn his love from others as well as himself. He loves neither others nor himself.

True love, the true life and fulfilment of God's will, is not one of selfishness but universal love, united with the life of humanity—past, present, and future. A life which we must live at this moment in time. True life is unselfish and is to be lived in the present. If we are not to fall by temptation, we must, at every moment of life, be at one with the will of God. When God's will shall become our choice, all things will be ours; life will be divested of its selfishness, and death disarmed of its terror.

To him who has understood that life consists in being, at this moment, in the grace of God, neither deprivation nor suffering, neither evil, nor death can be dreadful. To the Spirit no evil exists. Evil is but an illusion of life. Men who live by the spirit make up the kingdom of God.

Every man may, by his own effort, enter the kingdom of his Father, by submitting to His power, and fulfilling His will. Only he obtains true life who is, at every moment, ready to give up his bodily life in order to fulfil the will of God. Those who comprehend that they live, not through the body, but through the spirit, possess true life. The spirit is man's consciousness of his sonship to the infinite Spirit. The kingdom of God is in the soul of man, and all men who come to know they are sons of God receive true life.

Love and goodness towards one's fellow-men is the only true, free, eternal life. If eternal life in God is the only true life, and is in itself blessed, then it is so here in the world, in spite of all its sufferings.

> Oh how much more doth beauty beauteous seem
> By that sweet ornament which truth doth give!
> The rose looks fair, but fairer we it deem
> For that sweet odor which doth in it live.
> The canker-blooms have full as deep a dye
> As perfumèd tincture of the roses,
> Hang on such thorns, and play as wantonly
> When summer's breath their maskèd buds discloses.
> But, for their beauty only is their show,
> They live unwooed and unrespected fade;
> Die to themselves. Sweet roses do not so:
> Of their sweet deaths are sweetest odors made.[4]

Suffering
Transcending Good and Evil

Affliction is the school of virtue, as necessity is the mother of invention. The path to heaven leads through Hell. Struggle and conflict is in direct proportion to the knowledge of God. Pain, suffering and despair are a means to an end. The end being the awareness and consciousness of one's finite and infinite nature.

God, who is unconditional love, cannot choose us to suffer, unless either we are to receive from it a remedy to what is evil in ourselves, or else, as such, pain is a necessary part of the scheme of the Universe to restore us to the original perfection from which we have fallen.

The pain and sorrow that was the cause and occasion of so great a redemption lifts one to accept the pain and suffering of the human condition.

> Love thrives on inextinguishable pain,
> Which tears the soul, then knits the thread again.
> A mote of love exceeds all bounds; it gives
> The vital essence to whatever lives.
> But where love thrives, there pain is always found;
> Angels alone escape this weary round—
> They love without the savage agony.
> Which is reserved for vexed humanity.[1]

We must correctly interpret sufferings in order to enter into it, live it, and finally live beyond it. You are released from suffering when you realize the separate-self (ego) is only a figment of your imagination, and your deeper Self is within and beyond the process of existence and knows only freedom. Our true identity has always been and will always be one with the Supreme Identity.

Your Self is identical to the creative energy of which all things in the universe are a manifestation. Sin and suffering are caused by the separation of the soul from the Spirit. Resurrection is the reuniting of the soul with the Spirit. At the bottom of the soul is the soul of humanity itself. Grief and suffering become the catalysts for the wisdom of a generous heart.

> You do not become truly generous because you become rich. You become rich because you are truly generous.

Can it be that God allows evil in the world, not out of perversity or desire to harm, but because our suffering is the path to our salvation?

> Suffering may become a virtue if we allow it to be the instrument that will deliver us from evil and to dwell in Thy kingdom and glory forever and ever.

When evil exists and man is transformed by it, then evil must be perceived as necessary in the evolution of man's soul. If you are the cause of the evil, the offense carries its own form of punishment. It is evil only if it fails to uncover or bring about a Self-revelation that God and creation are of One immortal and eternal substance.

> It has been said unto you, An eye for an eye, and a tooth for a tooth: But I say unto you, That you resist not evil.
>
> Matthew 5:38-39

Evil becomes a reality when we choose to separate ourselves from the will of the Spirit. Any disharmonies which we experience are merely consequences of the choices we make. One must never do anything contrary to the law of love.

> An eye for an eye and we will all go blind.

He who fights with the sword must himself perish with the sword. We cannot obtain revenge by enlisting in the army of retribution. We merely perpetuate the evil. We must stand immune to the temptations of evil, regardless of what others are doing to us. By taking revenge against the injuries suffered at the hands of others, one is merely reinforcing the evil. Revenge is a common passion that enslaves man's mind and clouds his vision.

To the savage, revenge is a noble aspiration that makes him even with his enemies. In a civilized society that is seeking peace and harmony, it is a destructive force. Peace and harmony can be found only in spiritual elevation that reaches into every aspect of human life. It is the individual rebirth and rededication to the eternal principles of life.

Even in evil we can discern the rays of light and hope; for man may gradually come to see, in suffering and misery, the error of his ways. The appearance of evil is only our misperception due to the lack of a higher consciousness. Evil is only an illusion. If we were better attuned, we would not see evil; we would see only the evolution of everything we experience as good, and evil as simply the natural growth required for the spiritual unfoldment of our souls.

> Get behind Me, Satan! You are a stumbling
> block to Me; for you are not setting your mind
> on God's interests, but man's.

Matthew 16:23

Why is there evil? For the joy of good arising from it. Why darkness? That light may shine the more. Why suffering? For the instructions of the soul and the joy of sacrifice. Why the infinite play of creation and evolution? For love, truth, and beauty. For true bliss and pure joy.

Life, our existence in the world, is an uninterrupted succession of suffering and despair—from deprivations as well as from those of excess. From nature as well as from our own free will. The lessons of life tell us that nothing in the whole world is meaningless and suffering least of all. To regret one's own experiences is to arrest one's own development.

There is a palace that opens only to tears.[7]

He who can look at the beauty of the world and share in its tears, joys, pain, and sorrow realizes something of the wonder of both. He is in immediate contact with divine things and has gotten as near to God's secret as anyone, because behind joy and sorrow there is always a soul.

When Hallaj was in prison, he was asked, "What is love?" He answered: "You will experience it today and tomorrow and the day after tomorrow." That day they cut off his hands and feet. The next day they put him on the gallows, and the third day they gave his ashes to the wind....

Al-Hallaj

The most certain proof of love consists in suffering for the one we love. If one loves, he is freed from fear and all sufferings.

Jesus did not die "for our sins," Jesus died "because of our sins," and in that awareness begins the process towards our salvation.

Good and evil are the sources of all wisdom. In the elements of reality and the appearance of reality lie the divine forces of purification. Man must transcend these opposing forces in order to be able peacefully to live moment to moment in their presence.

Our salvation consists wholly in being saved from ourselves.

Pain and suffering, joy and bliss depend upon an unchangeable pattern, the forces of the natural order of the universe.

"I must accept whatever you bestow;
No harm can come to me from you, I know."
If you meet tribulations here be sure
That wealth will come from all you must endure;
The paths of God are intricate and strange—
What can you do? Accept what will not change![1]

If suffering by deprivation, excess, nature, or one's own free will is the means for transformation, then suffering must be perceived as necessary and good—for transformation is the creative evolutionary process from potentiality to realization.

When in disgrace with fortune and men's eyes,
I all alone beweep my outcast state,
And trouble deaf Heaven with my bootless cries,
And look upon myself, and curse my fate,
Wishing me like to one more rich in hope,
Featur'd like him, like him with friends possess'd,
Desiring this man's art, and that man's scope,
With what I most enjoy contented least;
Yet in these thoughts myself almost despising
Haply I think on thee,—and then my state,
(Like to the lark at break of day arising)
From sullen earth sings hymns at heaven's gate;
  For thy sweet love remember'd such wealth brings,
  That then I scorn to change my state with kings.[4]

Justice

We will not be satisfied until justice rolls down like waters and righteousness like a mighty stream.

Martin Luther King Jr. Book of Amos 5:24

Universal justice reveals itself differently to each individual, according to his own nature. Justice creates the condition in which each receives that which accords with his being, which is due him, and which constitutes the degree of his happiness and well-being.

> Forgive us our trespasses as we forgive those who trespass against us.

It is only pain and suffering that blame and punish us for our transgressions. Pain and suffering are not the punishment of evil but evil itself. Man reaps what he sows. God in His Divine Wisdom and Mercy could not inflict greater punishment, for man has already suffered, in being what he is. The law of God is that the consequences of wrong, cruelty, and crime shall be their punishment; and the injured and wronged are His instruments to enforce that law. There is no reason to judge, because God judges those by the quality of their actions.

> My teacher took me for a walk through the town one day. A man on a donkey would not make way for us in the narrow streets, and as we were slow in getting out of his path he cursed us roundly.
>
> "May he be punished for that behavior," people called out of their doorways.
>
> My teacher said to me, "How simple-minded people are! Little do they realize how things really happen. They only see one kind of cause and effect, while sometimes the effect, as they would call it, appears before the cause."

I was perplexed and asked him what he meant.

"Why," he said, "that man has already been punished for the behavior which he showed us just now.

"Last week he applied to enter the circle of the elite and was refused. Only when he realizes the reason will he be able to enter the circle of the elect. Until then he will continue to behave thus."

The offense carries its own form of punishment. He carries his own curse inside himself. The seeds of our punishment are sown at the time we commit the offense.

> The violence that others do to us is often less painful than violence we do to ourselves.
>
> La Rochefoucauld

When one has committed an offense against nature and his ego will not permit him to acknowledge and accept his transgression, then the defense of his actions— no matter how eloquent—is worse than the original offense itself. The ego will not accept that it is not infallible and rules supreme, thus causing an offense against the soul. The very defenses that man needs in order to move about with self-confidence and self-esteem become his life-long trap. We are never punished "for" doing something wrong; we are punished "by" doing something wrong. Its consequences are its punishment. The way of the transgressor is hard.

> He who commits injustice is made more wretched than he who suffers it.
>
> Plato

> A man whose job it was to keep the peace
> Beat up a drunk, who fought for his release
> And cried: "It's you who's tippled too much wine;
> Your rowdiness is ten times worse than mine—

Who's causing this disturbance, you or me?
But yours is drunkenness that men can't see;
Leave me alone! Let justice do its worst—
Enforce the law and beat yourself up first!"[1]

One must not judge or compare. One must delete the need to understand and cease the needless questioning why. One must surrender to his (His) existence.

Judge not, that ye be not judged. For with what judgment ye judge, ye shall be judged: and with what measure ye mete, it shall be measured to you again.

Matthew 7:1-2

One's whole life must be a spiritual struggle, to strive and exert oneself in the path of God. Only those having the courage to marshal one's armies and overcome the desires of the senses will experience the peace, love, and happiness that permeate the universe.

Blessed are the peacemakers for they shall be called the children of God.

Matthew 5:9

One must be a peacemaker to the mind's inner turmoil, so as to be able to become whole in God. One must purge and liberate the mind of all imperfections that foster the feelings that are evil. A mind which is beyond all images and multiplicities is one within itself and one in God. One must continually strive for inner purification. This is the fullness of reality, from becoming to "Being," from potentiality to "Reality."

Self-conquest is the greatest of victories.

Plato

Salvation's Lord is just,
And justice raises man above the dust;
To live with justice in your heart exceeds
A lifetime's earnest prayer and pious deeds;
And tales of lavish generosity
Are less than one just act done secretly
(Though justice given in a public place
Suggests deceit beneath the smiling face).
The just man does not argue for his rights;
It is for others that he stands and fights.[1]

The power, wisdom, and the justice of God are on the side of every just thought; it cannot fail, any more than God Himself can perish. Political structures change as do nations, but the life of man with its needs remains eternally the same. This cannot be changed. Life is inexhaustible. It exists for one and all. Generations come and go, and those that achieve a higher state of consciousness will enjoy life in its inexhaustible abundance.

A thing is not "Just" because God wills it; but
God wills it because it is "Just."

St. Thomas Aquinas

This Self-unfoldment enables man to fulfill his true destiny in the boundaries of time and space by experiencing love and immortality.

The destinies of men are subject to unchangeable laws that must fulfill themselves. Man has it in his power to shape his own destiny, according to the behavior he shows towards the influences of these benevolent and destructive forces.

Through a variety of human experiences, one is able to come to a realization that awakens and develops his higher nature by shaping his life through the use of his own power and free will, and, to move from the human to the supernatural dimension of existence.

He consciously moves with the cosmic current.
In moving he loses nothing but his limitations.
He can take with him in essence all the experiences
And understanding that he has gained.

Collins

Fate

There is a divinity that shapes our end,
Rough-hew them how we will.[4]

Nothing can make man lose his own essential nature, not even the adverse fate in the human condition. There is a special hand of providence in the fall of the sparrow. In such times there is nothing a man can do but accept his fate and transcend the suffering of the human condition and remain true to himself under all conditions and circumstances, for this alone is superior to all external fate.

There are more things in heaven and earth
Horatio than are dreamt of in your philosophy.

Hamlet
William Shakespeare

We human beings may be only the puppets of some supernatural force or other which we cannot possibly escape. The forces of the future. Our destiny.

The fates lead him who will; him who won't
they drag.

When difficulties and obstacles arise, they must be overcome by recognizing them for what they are. One must view life as a series of adventures and lessons. In recognizing as fate the things that must be so taken, one ceases to hate adversity.

Serenity Prayer

God, grant me the serenity to accept the things
I cannot change. Courage to change the things
I can and the wisdom to know the difference.

Of what use would it be to storm against fate? Through this lessening of resentment, character is purified and advances to a higher state of consciousness.

Death Speaks

There was a merchant in Bagdad who sent his servant to market to buy provisions and in a little while the servant came back, white and trembling, and said, Master, just now when I was in the market-place I was jostled by a woman in the crowd and when I turned I saw it was Death that jostled me. She looked at me and made a threatening gesture; now, lend me your horse, and I will ride away from this city and avoid my fate. I will go to Samarra and there Death will not find me. The merchant lent him his horse, and the servant mounted it, and he dug his spurs in the flanks and as fast as the horse could gallop he went. Then the merchant went down to the market-place and he saw me standing in the crowd and he came to me and said, Why did you make a threatening gesture to my servant when you saw him this morning? That was not a threatening gesture, I said, it was only a start of surprise. I was astonished to see him in Bagdad, for I have an appointment with him tonight in Samarra.

Somerset Maugham

Was the servant's journey to Samarra one of fate or one of free will? The answer is both. The universe is a whole. Each part is not isolated, but contains and reveals the whole. Complete determinism is equivalent to absolute freedom.

What I will is fate.   Milton

Did Jesus have free will, or was his free will determined by fate?

For he saw ere his eye was darkened
   The sheaves of the harvest-bringing,
And heard while his ears yet harkened
   The voice of the reapers singing.

Ah, well! the world is discreet;
    There are plenty to pause and wait;
But here was a man who set his feet
    Some time in advance of fate.

Life—it is like a man playing cards. There is the man himself and the cards he is playing and another man watching over his shoulder. The player is life, the watcher is the Spirit, and the cards are fate.

Fate has given me many a gift
    To which men most aspire.
Lovely, precious and costly things,
    But not my heart's desire.

Give me a soft and secret place
    Against thine amber breast,
Where hidden away from all mankind,
    My soul may come to rest.

*

The Winds of Fate

One ship drives east and another drives west
    With the selfsame winds that blow.
        'Tis the set of the sails
        And not the gales
Which tells us the way to go.

Like the wind of the sea are the ways of fate
    As we voyage along through life:
        'Tis the set of a soul
        That decides its goal,
    And not the calm or the strife.

                        Ella Wheeler Wilcox

The winds of Spirit are forever blowing.
Unfurl your sails!

States of Consciousness

Consciousness is simply stepping out of the darkness into the light.

Jesus the man, Christ the consciousness, said, "In my father's house there are many mansions." My interpretation of this profound statement is that these mansions are degrees of consciousness in all that exists. The higher the consciousness, the more the veil of mystery is lifted.

The kingdom of heaven is within man, and man experiences this kingdom to the degree that he becomes conscious of it. It is the conscious awareness of being attuned to something greater than oneself. Conscious awareness penetrates the mind's creation of the universe like a thread in a string of pearls. The thread represents the unchangeable reality pervading everywhere. It is the essence of "Being," one's true Self. The pearls represent multiplicity, the ever- changing reality of our finite existence.

Primitive Consciousness

There are five states of consciousness, five states of mind, that man must travel through. The first state of mind is called the pre-mind (the primitive unconscious mind). It exists in a very small child. The unconscious, chaotic, child-like state of an emotional nature is an animalistic nature of existence, unconscious of one's mortality.

At this stage, there is no center. Ignorance is the rule. The child is not able to listen. He thinks only of himself. The innocence, beauty, and grace of the child exists because that entity we call man has not evolved. The child is at ease. The child is not yet a traveler. He has not left his home in search of some other home. The pilgrimage has not started. The child is at rest, perfectly at ease and happy to be whatever he is.

That is why a child has a certain grace around him, but this grace will be lost because it is unconscious. It has not been earned. It is a natural gift, and the child is completely unaware of it.

This pre-mind is purely instinctive, natural, inherent in man's nature, and it must be transcended. He has not learned it. It is part of the wisdom of his body. There is no responsibility because the child knows nothing of duty, of values or of virtues. The child has no idea of heaven or hell, good or evil, right or wrong; so there is never any conflict. His desires are pure. He exists before the separation.

> Except ye be converted, and become as little children, ye shall not enter into the kingdom of heaven.
>
> Matthew 18:3

The child is not separated from his true nature. He does not perceive himself as anything else. He already is. Whenever he is in a certain mood, he is totally in it, but his moods are momentary. He has no identity. He is unpredictable. One moment he is loving and another moment he is angry. He is very inconsistent, because he is always unconsciously true to the moment. So the innocence is there, but not very deep. The child is more like an animal than like a man. The child is the link between the animal and the man.

Yet the child passes through all the stages man has passed through down the ages. Scientists say that in the mother's womb during the nine months the child passes through millions of years of creative evolution.

Even when the child is born he is still not a man. He has no idea what he is going to do. He has no concern for the future and no recollection of the past. He lives totally in the present moment. As the child grows in social consciousness, he loses his innocence and becomes part of the civilized world. He becomes man. To be like a child and yet be man enough to know its value is man's inevitable salvation.

Once he becomes man, he becomes separated from this grace, and that is when the search begins. Religion is nothing but the search for the lost and forgotten childhood, the soul's longing for the grace of God. The man who experiences the grace of God has eternal life. Everybody subconsciously carries the memory of this peace before the separation. A memory that will hallow all we have known and know no more, for memory is a midway world between earth and paradise.

> Harken to this Reed forlorn
> Breathing, even since, was torn
> From its rusty bed, a strain
> Of impassioned love and pain.
>
> The secret of my song, though near,
> None can see and none can hear.
> Oh, for a friend to know the sign
> And mingle all his soul with mine!
>
> 'Tis the flame of Love that fired me,
> 'Tis the wine of Love inspired me.
> Wouldst thou learn how lovers bleed,
> Hearken, hearken to the Reed.

Jalaludin Rumi

Man's soul is always yearning for something which is not of this world. It is the yearning for reunion with the origin of life. It is the quest for eternal beauty.

Collective-Social Consciousness

The first state of consciousness is chaotic. A child is very self-orientated and thinks only of himself. He is utterly selfish. The second state of consciousness is collective-social, one of communal solidarity. One thinks of others, but he is only able to give conditionally.

It is a selfish state, but there is a virtue in this type of selfishness. In this state of mind, blessedness is the reward for virtue rather than virtue itself. There is a false center. Blind faith is the rule. People in this state of consciousness hear the word of God, but do not understand.

In this state, a person starts sacrificing his own interest for those of others. He starts becoming responsible and civilized. He develops in social consciousness and loses his innocence by following the dictates of others, and thus becomes a part of the civilized world.

He learns that he is not an individual but a member of a society. He is influenced by his culture, schooling, family training, church, nation, and society. They all become an important part of his social-collective conscious mind.

The group, family, society, nation, and church become more important than the individual. Those in this group are capable of a mob mentality, which reveres a spiritual master today and is equally ready to tear him to pieces tomorrow.

The primitive mind has no identity at all. The collective mind has a certain identity. A person is this state of consciousness will say he belongs to a certain group, a certain ideology. "I am a Christian, a Jew, a Muslim, a Buddha, or a Hindu." Now he has an identity: "I am a doctor, an engineer, or a businessman. This is what I do, and this is my function in society."

This state is not one of Self-knowledge and Self-identity. It is one of a programmed self-identity.

Many people stop at the collective-social state of conscious development. If you stop at this state of mind, you will have taken on a false identity and will never know who you truly are. These labels you have acquired are only suitable in functioning as a member of society, but they do not tell you anything about your inner identity, your inner reality, your inner Self. You must realize that you exist on a far higher plane of consciousness.

You are a great promise. Do not let your pride delude you into thinking that you have achieved your goal, because a part of you will be pulled one way and another part will be pulled another way. You will be torn apart, you will remain in anguish, and your existence will be nothing but a long ongoing nightmare.

Pride goeth before destruction.

Proverbs 16:18

Everyone who is proud in heart is an abomination to the Lord.

Proverbs 16:5

And whoever exalts himself shall be humbled, and whoever humbles himself shall be exalted.

Matthew 23:12

This collective-social conscious mind is where almost everyone stops. Society does not want you to go beyond it. It has made you a member of the mass, a kind of slave. It has given you a certain imprisonment. It has taken away your freedom of choice, your individuality. It has made you dutiful and responsible and given you values of what is right or wrong. It has pigeonholed you, categorized you, and now you live silently in a routine existence until you die.

Man has become a beast of burden. He goes on carrying these heavy loads for no reason at all. He moves in a desert like a camel and carries these great loads. Even though these loads are crushing and killing him, he carries them just the same, because it has become a habit, a part of his definition and his anxiety. Then sadness and misery become part of his identity. His normal condition becomes a sickness.

These camels you will find everywhere and this desert is all over the earth. The child must move from the first state of consciousness to the second, but must not stop there.

A man is respected if he is carrying great loads of responsibility, duty, family, and society; but at this state of collective responsibility and social consciousness, he has sacrificed his whole being. He has lost the freedom of his individuality. To be a camel is not the goal. You will have gained respect and honor if you are a good camel and carry great loads, but something more is needed.

In this state of consciousness man has not acquired personal responsibility yet. In the first state of consciousness, the child has no responsibility. In the second state of consciousness the responsibility is collective. You feel responsible only because you are a part of a certain collectivity, a certain group.

All function according to their community, and according to the rules. Nobody has any responsibility to think for himself. The rules have been given to each of us. Even in the scriptures, everything is clear cut. There is no need to speculate, philosophize, wonder, or to meditate. All problems have been solved for you.

The collective-social mind is not rebellious or tense, because it lacks the awareness that it is suffering—the awareness of an individual anxiety in which to rebel. Society lives in the acceptance of the normal condition, even though it is a sickness.

The peace of the collective-social mind is not very creative, but it is good in a way. One lives one's life without much anguish, but nothing comes out of that life. It is peaceful, but never creative. The false sense of peace is there because there is a feeling of belonging to a group, belonging to a community, belonging to a religious institution.

Nobody feels alone or anxious because everything has been programmed for him. His identity has been given to him by others. This is a kind of fatalism. All that has happened must be accepted, because it cannot be otherwise. If it cannot be otherwise, why worry?

This is not a good state of consciousness even though there are fewer psychological breakdowns at this state. The collective-social state of mind is a kind of patriarchy, the father figures remain very important. This is a finite consciousness of an authoritarian existence of conditional and transitory love where disobedience must be overcome with punishment, repentance and submission.

> I am a very jealous God. If you go against me
> I will destroy you.
>
> Joshua 24:19-20

The collective-social mind is repressive and does not allow you to be an individual. People believe in God because they are told to believe in God. People go to church because they have been told to go to church. People do things ritualistically because of their culture or background. Jesus called these people hypocrites.

One must not live a life of an imposter. An imposter is all a man is when he fails to be true to the things he believes in.

Be careful not to parade your good deeds before men to attract their notice; by doing this you will lose all reward from your Father in heaven.

So when you give alms, do not have it trumpted before you; this is what the hypocrites do in the synagogues and in the streets to win mens admiration. I tell you solemnly, they have had their reward.

But when you give alms, your left hand must not know what your right hand is doing.

Your almsgiving must be in secret, and your Father who sees all that is done in secret will reward you.

And when thou prayest, thou shalt not be as the hypocrites are: for they love to pray standing in the synagogues and on the street corners, in order to be seen by men. Verily I say unto you, They have their reward.

But thou, when thou prayest, go into your inner room, and when you have shut your door, pray to your Father who is in secret, and your Father who seeth in secret shall reward thee openly.

But when ye pray, use not vain repetitions, as the heathen do: for they think that they shall be heard for their much speaking.

Be not ye therefore like unto them: for your Father knoweth what things ye have need of, before ye ask him.

After this manner therefore pray ye:

Our Father which art in heaven, Hallowed be thy name, Thy kingdom come. Thy will be done in earth, as it is in heaven. Give us this day our daily bread. And forgive us our debts, as we forgive our debtors. And lead us not into temptation, but deliver us from evil. For thine is the kingdom, and the power, and the glory, for ever.

Matthew 6:1-13

It is the confession not the priest that gives us absolution.

The collective-social state of mind has only a painted exterior, the interior remains untouched, unresolved. It is a kind of theism. People believe in God, in heaven and hell, punishment and reward. These people believe, but they do not know.

They hear the word of God, but they do not understand. They follow only, because their belief has been forced upon them. True belief, based on an inner revelation, has not been given a chance to evolve and unfold within them. There is a communal solidarity, because they are never alone. They think because so many people are going in the same direction, they cannot all be wrong; so they must be right by going along with them. Although the moment they are alone, anxiety arises.

It is essential to them that other people follow the same rules they have, because they cannot fully believe their sacrifices will work for them unless the same system works for other people. Their resentment goes towards those who ignore their rules and still seem to find a sense of peace.

Individual Consciousness

The third mind is the individual conscious mind. The independent, assertive, rebellious mind realizes that it is suffering. The ego has evolved and become very crystallized. It is unwilling to be satisfied with the purely animal or the purely collective-social state of consciousness. Man is no longer a part of a collective-social group, that follows the dictates of others. He rejects collective-social consciousness in order to assert his individuality. He experiences the freedom of choice and its consequences. He is an individual with a sense of Self. His identity is more personal, more creative. This mind is not one of belonging, but of contributing.

By and by a center arises in the individual's conscious mind. In the child mind there was no center. In the collective mind there was a false center, imposed by others from the outside. In the individual mind an inner center arises. All scriptures and Jesus' sayings are addressed to the individual conscious mind (the ego mind).

He that be without sin cast the first stone.

John 8:7

Only here is understanding possible. Ego has a certain function to fulfill. It is a necessary step. The collective-social mind cannot understand the suffering of the ego.

Suffering can bring you to a higher state of consciousness than this false sense of peace. Suffering can be very creative. As a skilled artist makes an image of wood or stone, he or she does not place the image within the wood but chisels away the pieces that have hidden and covered it up. The work of the artist is to carve out and unveil the glory that is hidden in creation.

The artist contributes nothing to the wood or stone, but takes away and removes the covering (veil) and takes away the blight (imperfections and contaminations); and what lay hidden underneath shines forth (love, truth and beauty). This is the treasure (The kingdom of God) that lays hidden in the field (soul). The pearl of great worth. The chiselling to perfection is not unlike that of the suffering needed in the process of man's purification—one of removing the blight and imperfections that contaminate the soul.

If you are suffering from a disease, the medicine, the remedy, becomes significant. If you are not suffering from a disease, the remedy has no value for you. If an ill man thinks he is already healthy, why should he listen to any doctor. And then there is no possibility of his illness being treated. The collective-social mind has not suffered yet from the ego; hence, anything that helps to go beyond ego is meaningless. It has no point of reference. Jesus talks to the third mind. If you are still in the second mind, Jesus will remain an enigma to you. The collective-social mind has no understanding; it is imitative and has no individual identity.

The collective-social conscious mind is one of following a religion about Jesus, instead of following the religion of Jesus. An inner center arises but doubt is the rule. One hears the word of God, understands the word of God, but is unable to follow.

Once intellectual understanding has flowered, will the door to wisdom then open? Yes, the universal mind follows only when the ego has suffered and has been dropped. The suffering is necessary to remove the blight and imperfections that contaminate the soul. The ego in the individual mind, when developed, can be dropped.

> How to get rid of the lower self: The blossom vanishes of itself as the fruit grows, so will your lower self vanish as the divine grows in you.

The ego drops by itself if it has served its purpose and made available the fourth door, the cosmic-universal mind. The function of religion is to make you aware that the fourth door exists and is forever available. It is the universal kiss. Like gravity, God's presence is always there; and, if you make yourself available, He will act upon you. God will kiss you and make Himself known to you. The universal kiss is a gift of love, a gift available only to those who are willing to receive it. Those who do not receive this gift of love are self-condemned.

Only when the ego function has been fulfilled will man go beyond the individual mind to cosmic-universal consciousness. The social mind is a collective neurosis, and the individual mind is a private neurosis. Only when the individual mind has transcended the suffering of the ego will the cosmic-universal conscious mind be able to follow.

The primitive mind was a kind of chaos with no order. The collective mind was a kind of patriarchy—an imposed order by the demanding society and its father figures. The individual mind is a kind of fraternity. Not one of master nor servant, but one of concern for others. A brotherhood arises. You do not belong to any club. Nobody can impose anything upon you. You entertain and utter your own convictions and leave everyone else free to do the same. You respect the freedom of others as much as you respect your own. All are brothers. Each exists independently of each other and yet co-exists interdependently with each other.

The trouble with the ego, the separate-self, is that it is derived from others. It needs support. Somebody needs to appreciate it. Somebody needs to say to you that you are a beautiful person. Some one needs to go on feeding it. It exists only in society. It is constructed to live up to the expectation of others.

The ego is not you; it belongs to others. It exists in you, but it is possessed by others. That is why it is so easy to manipulate an egoist person. Society is very clever. It tries to keep you at the collective-social conscious level. If you go beyond that, then it starts manipulating and controlling you through flattery and imitation.

As an individual, a very personal responsibility arises within you. You start feeling responsible for your actions, because now you know what is right or wrong. You have freedom of choice.

> It is not what you ought to say, but what you feel.

With a greater understanding, consciousness evolves. There is more joy, because you will be more of an individual; but there will also be more anxiety too. Now if something goes wrong, you alone are responsible for it. You cannot look at a father figure and you cannot throw your responsibility onto somebody else. You are alone. You are now responsible for your own actions. With these responsibilities arise great anxieties and tensions. Each choice has to be decisive, because you cannot go back in time. This is the state of mind where people start having psychological breakdowns.

In the primitive mind, ignorance was the rule. In the collective mind, faith was the rule. In the individual mind, doubt becomes the rule. Where there is freedom, there is tension. Rebellion cannot exist without the individualistic mind. And the ego cannot grow and ripen without the individualistic mind. You have to rebel to the sickness of the normal human condition, so that your rebellion may become significant.

This rebellion is a very creative crisis, because if you go above the individual mind, it will be creative. When you have tasted the freedom of individuality and are very conscious of it, you cannot go back to the faith of the collective-social conscious mind. A man who has doubted, and who has experienced the freedom of his will, cannot go back to blind faith again. If he does, then the faith will be simple cunningness and deception. He will not be able to deceive himself as he had in the past. He has gone beyond.

Man is never deceived; he deceives himself.

Goethe

If in the individual state of consciousness there is a possibility of surrendering the ego, then the ego is of immense value; but the value is in its surrender. If you cannot surrender the ego function, then it will become a great burden to you. It will become unbearable and you will go on roaring like a lion, seeking peace that is beyond your reach.

The individual mind is in the center and at its most critical stage. The collective-social mind is below and the cosmic-universal mind is above it. It is exactly the mid-link. The individual conscious mind faces two possibilities, either he can go up and become one with the whole, or fall back and become one with the collective-social conscious mind that has not created the ego yet. If you fall, you become miserable. If you rise, you obtain supreme blessedness.

You cannot attain a cosmic-universal state of awareness without first passing through the individual conscious state of mind. These are the complexities. If you try to avoid the third door (the individual conscious mind), you will remain stuck to the collective-social mind and you will think it is the cosmic-universal mind. It is not; it is simply collective. If you feel trapped, you will become miserable. You may even remain in the primitive conscious mind, which is idiotic and in societies the idiotic looks much like the saintly. There are some similarities between the idiot and the saint. They are both without mind, but are widely separated. The idiot is below mind and the Christ (the saint) is above mind, but both are beyond mind. That is the only similarity.

The primitive mind is not the goal; it is the beginning. The collective mind is very comfortable, but not truly happy. Comfort is not the question. The individual mind is creative, but uncomfortable, very anxious and tense, a maverick, forever searching. How long can you remain creative when there is so much tension? The tension must be lost. Hence, the cosmic-universal conscious mind. In the cosmic-universal mind, all is silent. Just the last lingering of the ego remains. If one feels and thinks he is one with the whole then one must get rid of that idea if he is to "be" totally "one" with the whole. This is the last barrier. Then his ego is completely lost.

Cosmic-Universal Consciousness

The individual mind has to be transcended in order to be conscious of the cosmic-universal mind. Cosmic-universal consciousness begins to touch an awareness that transcends the individual and discloses to a person something which passes far beyond himself. The separation with the cosmos has to disappear. You have to come to the realization that you are one with the universe. The ego does not want to be part of anything but itself. It feeds on itself; and until you suffer and the ego dies, you will never experience your true Self.

Paradoxically, suffering and the movement into isolation and loneliness ultimately will lead man back to the collective-social community with the love of God for all mankind. He moves from dependence to independence to an autonomy defined in the context of interdependence.

Many who have learned to embrace their independence have developed a strong enough sense of Self that they are not afraid of being swallowed up by the collective-social condition.

No matter how much man wants to feel loved, appreciated, and a part of the collective-social conscious mind, there will be loneliness deep in his soul until he makes a commitment to himself as an individual—a commitment that is so total that he will give up community and love, if necessary, to achieve the fullness of his true nature and experience the transcendental conscious mind. An experience that is so total that he will be fully conscious of who he is and has always been.

> He who loves father or mother more than
> me is not worthy of me;
>
> And he who loves son or daughter more
> than me is not worthy of me;
>
> And he who does not take his cross and
> follow after me is not worthy of me.
>
> He who has found his life shall lose it, and
> he who has lost his life for my sake shall find it.

Matthew 10:37-39

When the cosmic-universal conscious mind comes into bloom, there is great joy. You have disappeared and all the energy that was involved in the ego is freed. That energy now becomes love, truth, and beauty.

The collective-social mind is Patriarchal, the individual mind is Fraternal and the cosmic-universal mind is Matriarchal. Mother's love is not demanding. Such is the love of the universe towards you. It demands nothing. It is unconditional. It is forever showering on you. It is there for you to accept or not to accept.

The individual mind transcends itself. Having tasted for a moment ultimate (God) consciousness, it attains a state of "Being." Man ceases to be an individual with an egoist mind and becomes one with the cosmic-universal conscious mind. He now thinks of others, and his giving is unconditional.

> I give nothing as duties. What others give as
> duties, I give as living impulses.

Walt Whitman

One in cosmic-universal solidarity thinks of others with unselfish motives. He will live in the field of action and yet spontaneously live a life of eternal freedom in the blissful consciousness of absolute "Being." He will live and act with full interest in the world, yet simultaneously live in God-consciousness, thereby bringing the values of the absolute into his relative state of existence.

With unconditional giving, the forces of our perceived reality will have had a glimpse of the transcendental conscious mind. Man will become aware that this state of ultimate (God) consciousness is certainly better in its unlimited state of absolute bliss than in the relative state of transitory happiness.

From that moment on his nature will have been changed and transformed to one of a much higher state of consciousness, and he will live dialectically in both realities at the same time. An inner center of peace arises and becomes the rule. He hears the word of God, understands the word of God, and is able to follow.

Transcendental Consciousness

There is a very thin veil, almost transparent, between the cosmic-universal mind and the transcendental mind. When that veil is lifted you will enter a transcendental state of consciousness, where you will have disappeared. It is by its very nature a paradoxical state, for it is empty and at the same time fills you with the bliss of eternal solitude. The mystical ecstasy of salvation. Ecstasy is its own reward, an end in itself. In such ecstasy all dualism dies, all separation ceases. Ecstasy recovers the primordial freedom and bliss of the ages that existed before time—a dream that has obsessed the human spirit from the beginnings of its history.

That moment of emptiness is what Jesus calls the kingdom of God, and Buddha calls Nirvana. It is to be totally one with the essence of existence.

> Enter ye in at the strait gate: for wide is the gate, and broad is the way, that leadeth to destruction, and many there be which go in thereat:

> Because strait is the gate, and narrow is the
> way, which leadeth unto life, and few there be
> that find it.
>
> Matthew 7:13-14

The majority follow the wide gate. That is why you do not see flowering and moments of spontaneity.

One must go in through the narrow gate, because the gate to hell is wide and the road that leads to it is easy, and there are many who travel it. But the gate to Life is narrow and the way that leads to it is hard and there are few people who find it. One has to go on until the goal is reached.

The wide gate is the gate of the senses and the narrow gate is the gate of the spirit that the soul enters in order to journey into the heart of pure consciousness, the means whereby the soul is united to the source of existence.

Both gates look alike, but there is a great difference; and the difference is if you go downwards the gate is wide but if you go upwards, narrow is the way. You must enter the narrow gate and walk on a narrow path. You cannot take anyone with you. That is why meditation and prayer have to be done in solitude. You must walk it alone.

> Jesus walked this lonesome valley.
> He had to walk it by Himself.
> No one else could walk it with Him.
> He had to walk it all alone.
>
> You have to walk this lonesome valley.
> You have to walk it by yourself.
> No one there to go it with you.
> You have to walk it all alone.
>
> Spiritual

Not I—Not anyone else, can travel the road for you,
you must travel it for yourself.

Walt Whitman

The higher you go the more you walk alone. The lower you go the more you are with a crowd of people. It is like a pyramid—the lowest part of the pyramid has the biggest base. As you go higher the pyramid gets smaller and narrower; at the apex it is just a point. Beyond this point is transcendental (pure) consciousness.

The primal is the base of the pyramid, the collective higher, the individual even higher still. When the individual reaches the cosmic-universal and goes beyond the apex, the pyramid disappears and the fifth mind, the transcendental conscious mind, comes into being. It is not part of the pyramid at all.

What is the similarity between the transcendental cosmic-universal mind and the collective-social mind? The cosmic-universal mind has transcended the ego. It is in tune with the whole. The collective mind has not created the ego yet. It is in tune with the social, but both have a kind of atonement (at-one-ment). The collective mind is at ease with society. It is adjusted with society and has become its victim.

An important goal of childhood development and education is the utilization of the individual in the sense of making him a useful member of the community. This usefulness is achieved by changing the individual to conform to the needs of society.

A steady loss of the vitality of feeling and of spontaneous reactions in the interest of "sensibleness" and "good behavior" is the normal conduct now demanded of the child in relation to the collective-social mind. Wholeness is exchanged for a workable and successful false personality.

Whenever somebody becomes too much of an individual, the psychoanalysts say he is maladjusted; then they attempt to bring him back to the collective-social state of mind. They help you to adjust to the normal condition, that which they call normal health. The collective mind will simply help you to remain adjusted, calm, quiet and "uniform," but there will be no ecstasy. It reduces tension. It makes you comfortable and secure, but at a great cost.

Let ecstasy be the criterion. If you follow the wide gate your ecstasy is diminished. Whenever you follow the narrow gate your ecstasy will grow.

Institutional religions remain stuck at the collective-social conscious state of mind and remain adjusted to the society. A true religion is one that helps the individual to go beyond the collective mind. That is the difference between psychoanalysis and religion.

A true religious belief will also make you adjusted, not with the society but with God and Self. That is real adjustment and a great joy arises out of it. To be adjusted with society is not the most desirable arrangement. You will be less tense, but not very happy. The cosmic-universal transcendental conscious mind will give you joy, bliss, and a celebration.

The West with its excesses needs urgently to enter the fourth door. If man's ego will not let him find the fourth door (the cosmic-universal conscious mind), he will be lost. The hunger is there but the ego is in the way and in control.

The ego is necessary, but one must not confine himself to it. Once the ego is transcended, man will be one with the Source of all existence. Only then will the great beatitudes arise. This is something that goes higher than deity. If you can experience this love, truth, and beauty then life has served its purpose and given it meaning.

We must be willing to discard the ego, the personality. God is no respecter of persons. God loves individuals, but not persons and the difference is great.

> A great Zen teacher was the head of Tofuku, a cathedral in Kyoto. One day the governor of Kyoto called upon him for the first time.
>
> His attendant presented the card of the governor, which read: Kitagaki, Governor of Kyoto.
>
> "I have no business with such a fellow," said the Zen teacher to his attendant. "Tell him to get out of here."
>
> The attendant carried the card back with apologies. "That was my error," said the governor, and with a pencil he scratched out the words Governor of Kyoto. "Ask your teacher again,"
>
> "Oh, is that Kitagaki?" exclaimed the teacher when he saw the card. "I want to see that fellow."

The personality is only a mask. It is a theatrical creation, a mere stage prop. The longing for absolute freedom, salvation or nirvana, means simply to be relieved of your so-called personality, the mask and the prison it creates.

> All the world's a stage, And all the
> Men and women merely players;
> They have their exits and their entrances;
> And one man in his time plays many parts.[4]

Go deep into the mirror of reality and behold things as they truly are and the masquerade will be over. There is no real difference between God and His creation. Only their costumes differ. On the stage one person plays a beggar, another a king; while the king commands respect and obedience, the beggar and his language evoke pity.   But there is no beggar or king in the greenroom; both are actors earning the same wage.

Similarly, God is the whole creation while you and I are only limited beings. Because of our costumes, we appear to be different.   These appearances do not represent real differences.   Those possessing God consciousness are one with the absolute, the one who plays all roles. The limitations belong to the body and not to the Self.

> The universe will fade—this mighty show
> In all its majesty and pomp will go.[1]

One transcends himself when he realizes the truth of his situation and dispels the lie of his character, by breaking his spirit out of its conditioned prison.

This happens when man succeeds in acquiring all of the masks that people use to bluff the world and themselves against the fear of death; and, as time passes, he comes to realize that these substitute gods were not what was really needed. They were only strategies and techniques for maintaining his self-esteem in the face of the terror of death.

These techniques become an armor that holds man prisoner. These substitute gratifications will not bring him fulfillment or complete happiness, and it is this realization that is often very devastating; one is wrecked with one's own success.

When one becomes aware of his situation, he will transcend all of the false masks that he uses to deceive himself and the world, and rise to a higher state of consciousness. This person will see the world in all its awe and splendor, and sense the expansion of his own free inner Spirit. Wherever he turns he will see the face of God.

When we see the all-pervading unity behind and beyond the masks of creation, we see our divinity—the miracle of His "Being."

> The zebra is an invisible animal, striped black
> and white, so you can see it coming.

Under the surface we are one. The visible is a measure of the invisible. The names and images for God are many and the masks of eternity both cover and reveal "the face of glory" that lies beyond the visible world, signifying the ultimate reality that transcend the illusions of time and space. This is a mysticism that calls us to a deeper awareness of the very act of living itself.

The Drug Sub-Culture

Those in the drug culture have dropped out of the normal process of living (the normal process of spiritual elevation) and created a world of their own. Those in this group have not attained the individual state of consciousness necessary for the spiritual evolution of their soul. They have created their own collective-social sub-culture. It has almost the same structure as the collective-social order they condemn and are attempting to avoid.

In the old social structure you cannot have long hair. In their social order, you cannot have short hair. The old structure is the same, but it is too conventional. You will look anti-social to your group if you have short hair. But it is the same type of collective-social order and structure. Even though it is rebellious, this type of rebellion is not creative. It is not one that strives for a higher state of consciousness. It merely repositions itself in the same collective-social structure. It is not going beyond mind to be at peace with itself. It is merely rebelling for the sake of rebellion. This counter-culture lifestyle is an orphaned generation that is going against one collective-social order and structure while creating another. This does not bring about a true sense of peace.

There is a big difference between a spiritually elevated person and one who has attained cosmic-universal consciousness by the use of drugs. With the use of drugs, one temporarily bypasses the individual consciousness of the ego state "and its suffering" to experience the cosmic-universal mind. This state of mind has a sense of peace but a false sense of security, because, once the drugs are withdrawn, this person falls back to the collective-social state of mind that he rebelled against, and the vicious cycle of drug elevation, to attain spiritual consciousness, is continued until he realizes that this is only a temporary solution to his problems.

Those using drugs are ones who have not as yet renounced their ego. Their suffering has not reached the point where the ego can effectively be dropped for something greater.

A spiritual person is one in whom the ego evolved and was dropped. He has gone beyond the collective-social mind, beyond the rebellious individual egoistic mind, and is one with the cosmic-universal conscious whole. A spiritual person is moving away from the very "need" to be part of any collective-social group.

To follow the path of the spiritual person, the God-, Christ- or Buddha-consciousness within, one will have to start dropping his ego. Then the cosmic-universal mind will flower within, and you will be able to follow.

Prayer and meditation are the only ways to peace, not drugs and uncontrolled sex. When the cosmic-universal conscious mind has unfolded, do not stop there. One step more is needed. This very consciousness that you have attained; this very consciousness by which you have realized God; this very consciousness that you have become one with the whole—all these have to be dropped, too. This is the last barrier. Once the barrier has been surpassed, you and the whole are "One." One body. One mind. One consciousness. A transcendental state of consciousness. That is what Jesus calls the kingdom of heaven.

Abide with me, fast falls the eventide;
The darkness deepens, Lord, with me abide.
When other helpers fail, and comforts flee,
Help of the helpless, O abide with me!

Swift to the close ebbs out life's little day;
Earth's joys grow dim, its glories pass away;
Change and decay in all around I see,
O Thou who changest not, abide with me!

I need Thy presence every passing hour,
What but Thy grace can foil the tempter's power?
Who like Thy-Self my guide and stay can be?
Thru cloud and sunshine, O abide with me!

Hold Thou Thy cross before my closing eyes,
Shine thru the gloom, and point me to the skies;
Heaven's morning breaks, and earth's vain shadows flee—
In life, in death, O Lord, abide with me![12]

*The haloed "Lamb of God" holds
Latin cross for atonement*

Summary

Transcendental	An Unutterable Source of Existence
Cosmic-universal.	Spirit—Love, Truth and Beauty—Grace
Individual	Ego—Becoming
Collective-social	Institutional
Primitive	Animal nature

The primitive state of consciousness is emotional and chaotic. The collective-social state is intellectual. The individual state is intelligence where intellect comes to its peak. Cosmic-universal state of consciousness is intuitive. It is a love of the heart. Love starts flowing and life is lived according to love and not according to logic. Love is the universal kiss. If you make yourself available, the universal mother will kiss you, embrace you and take you again into her womb.

In the primitive conscious mind there is no center. There is a kind of chaos, with no order, ignorance is the rule, and one is not able to listen.

In the collective-social conscious mind there is a kind of Patriarchy imposed by others from the outside by a demanding society and its father figures. It has a false center. Blind faith is the rule. One is able to listen and he hears the word of God, but is unable to understand or follow.

In the individual conscious mind an inner center arises and doubt becomes the rule. It is a kind of fraternity, one of concern for others. A brotherhood arises. The individual hears the word of God, understands the word of God, but is unable to follow. Once intellectual understanding has arisen, then the fourth door opens. Only the cosmic-universal mind can follow.

In the cosmic-universal conscious mind an inner center of peace arises and peace becomes the rule. The cosmic-universal mind lives in Truth. It is not belief. It is not what someone has forced you to believe. It is your own vision. It is not imposed on you from the outside. It comes from the innermost core of your Being. It is your own inner experience. It is one in cosmic-universal solidarity, where one thinks of others with unselfish motives. One hears the word of God, understands the word of God, and is also able to follow.

Moses brought the primitive mind to a civilized collective-social state of consciousness. Jesus brought the collective-social mind to an individual state of consciousness. As an individual "You" must take yourself from the individual conscious state of mind to the cosmic-universal state of consciousness and you must go it alone.

In the transcendental conscious mind the ego is totally dropped. The masks of creation and the prison it creates will have disappeared. There is no subject or object. You are totally one with the essence of existence.

When you can become a witness of God, there is true religion. It has become your own existential experience. Solidarity again enters but solidarity with existence itself and not with society. Creativity comes again, but not in the form of an egoistic creativity.

God flows through you. You now live in this world dialectically, serving and being one with your God-given nature. You cannot create great music or poetry without it.

> Mathematics is the music and poetry of the mind. Music and poetry is the mathematics of the soul.

Mathematics, philosophy, and science are concerned with the mind. Poetry and music are concerned with the heart. Religion is concerned with just "Being."

When you come to the cosmic-universal conscious mind, great creativity is born. Your very touch becomes creative. One must learn this art. Man carries his own heaven or hell within. It is only a matter of perception. The world is as you see it. It can be heaven, or it can be hell.

> A famous soldier came to the Master and asked, "Master, tell me! Is there really a heaven and a hell?" "Who are you?" asked the Master. "I am a samurai warrior of the great emperor's personal guard," replied the soldier. "Nonsense!" said the Master. "What kind of emperor would have you as his guard? To me, you look like a beggar!" At this, the soldier started to rattle his big sword in anger. "Oho!" said the Master. "So you have a sword! I will wager it is much too dull to cut off my head!" At this, the soldier could not hold himself back. He drew his sword and threatened the Master, who said, "Now you know half the answer! You are opening the gates to Hell!" At these words the samurai soldier, perceiving the master's teachings, drew back and sheathed his sword and bowed. "Please forgive me," he said. "Now you know the other half of the answer," said the Master, "You now have opened the gates to Heaven."

The truth of this wisdom is that man is responsible for his own actions, and he is the source and means of his own folly and the source and means of his own Salvation. We are the determinant that shapes inner and outer reality.

The day you know how to see rightly you will have learned the art of turning the whole world into gold. That is the secret of alchemy.

What we experience in our lives, both good and evil, is there for us to realize the God-consciousness within us. Our life will become glorious by the way we perceive good and evil. Will the passions of the world foster compassion that will enable us to effectively relate to the joys and suffering of others?

There is no such thing as absolute reality in our relative world. It is all a question of perception. The way we perceive the events in our lives is everything. We are not the victims of the world we see, but we are the victims of the way we see the world.

When you enter the cosmic-universal mind, the veil of matter will have been removed, and you will be conscious of the presence of God. The true progress of man on earth will be the awareness of an inner vision that leads to the heart, one of love and Self-realization through the bliss of self-transcendence.

You are now capable of true creativity, but as a humble servant of God and not as a servant of an egoistic mind. You become a hollow bamboo and His song starts descending through you. God turns you into a flute and the music within your soul will be according to the capacity you have to receive Him.

One's journey now is to return to the center. It is a childhood again, but a second childhood. It is one of conscious awareness—a state of grace—and one of love, where you will understand the hidden mysteries and secrets of eternity.

> We are born into the world of nature; our second birth is into the world of spirit.

> Bhagavad Gita.

Your life is transformed. There is innocence, intelligence, and love, but all are coming from your innermost center. Your inner fountain is flowing.

Misery, darkness, anxiety, and tension will have disappeared. The nightmare will be over. You are now fully awake. In that wakefulness is sainthood.

When you have gone beyond the cosmic-universal mind, you have transcended time and space. There is no subject or object. You are beyond mind. If you are still conscious of your surroundings and that you are one with the whole, then the unity is not yet total. When you have transcended, you will be in a state of "Being," one of consciousness and bliss, where there is no separation. You will be utterly conscious and fully aware.

Jesus' Claim to Divinity

Jesus' claim for divinity is a claim for the divinity of us all. We must become aware that his relationship to God is a pattern which all of us must follow and one day attain. It is the awareness of the atonement (at-one-ment) in God, the soul of us all. As spiritual beings we are to become One with God, no separation, no unresolved estrangement from the Spirit. There is but One God!

Hear, O Israel: the Lord thy God is One!

Deuteronomy 6:4

There is no god but God.   Quran

Jesus is the fruit and the flower of all Jewish history. If you are just a Christian, a Muslim, a Buddhist, a Hindu, or a Jew then you will not be able to understand Jesus. The people who gathered around Jesus must have been very individualistic people; otherwise, how was it possible for them to listen to somebody who was so rebellious, who was such a radical? He was turning the whole society upside down, saying continuously, "It has been told to you in the old days, but I say unto you," and then was denying all that had been said. He was continuously dismantling and destroying. Only a few individual, rebellious people must have gathered around him.

Jesus the man; Christ the consciousness. One must believe in the supremacy of God the Father, and in the humanity and divine missions of Jesus of Nazareth.

Somehow he gets thoughtful sitting by himself so much, and thinks the strangest things you ever heard. He told me that he hoped the people saw him in the church, because he was a cripple, and it might be pleasant to them to remember upon Christmas Day, who made lame beggars walk, and blind men see.

Tiny Tim, Christmas Carol, Charles Dickens

Social redemption, divine grace, and the salvation of man's soul is affected by the change in the heart and life wrought by the Christ spirit.

My faith is simply this—that there is an original corruption in our nature, from which and from the consequences of which we may be redeemed by Christ, not by his pure morals, or excellent example merely—but in a mysterious manner as an effect of his Crucifixion.

Samuel Taylor Coleridge

We are all men just as Jesus was, but Christ represented Divine-consciousness; and, in this light, we, too, can become Christ-conscious if we transcend the lower levels of consciousness and cease identifying with them. We must raise our consciousness from the lowest to the highest level to reach the omega point wherein all souls reawaken to Ultimate (God) consciousness.

Man is mind. Biological man is not a being, but a passage from the primal chaotic mind towards the transcendental conscious mind, a highly elevated form of consciousness. The mind and the body are transient and only instruments of divine love. Those who reach a higher state of consciousness are able to fine tune their biological instrument, the mind, to an elevated state of consciousness, experiencing the divine flow, as the scientist fine tunes his instruments to enable him to comprehend that which is unseen. It is truly the destiny, freedom, and the immortality of man's soul to enter into full consciousness with God.

> Might we create of the twin, one new being and
> in so doing, being One in many.

There is no rest in being a man. Man is a journey between two infinities; one is your nature, and another is your hidden God. Man is a link, just in-between. Man has to be surpassed. Man has to be transcended. Man is a ferry boat. You must go beyond. Then the boat can be left behind.

The teachings of most religions and those of Jesus show how to go beyond man. That is why Jesus says again and again, "I am the son of man and son of God." He goes on insisting on this contradiction because he wants it to be completely clear that man is both, a part of nature and part of God.

Faith embraces many apparently contradictory truths. Is man a God? Jesus said, "I and God are one." "I and man are one." "I am the son of God." "I am the son of man." True faith embraces the humanity of man and the divinity of God.

As long as man is separated by these two natures, these two realities, there will be no rest for him. There will be constant anxiety, tension and inner conflict. As a man there is no possibility of peace. Either man becomes completely unconscious like a drunkard, where he has lost all sense of his consciousness, or he will have to become so conscious that his total Being will be full of light.

Only when your consciousness becomes a Buddha or a Christ will there be peace. You either have to fall below man or go beyond man. A conscious being is never just what it is; it falls below the level of its capacity, or it reaches out beyond its actual state of expectations.

Do not go on desiring and clinging to being a man, because then you are clinging to a disease (dys-ease). Life is a constant tension to be or not to be, to be one with man or to be one with God.

You must let go of man as such, and start thinking how to go beyond, how to transcend, how to surpass man. This is the breakthrough. It is the greatest miracle in the world for man to surpass himself. It has happened to Christ, Krishna, Muhammad, Chuang-tse, Lao-tse, Buddha and to many others. It can happen in you.

> To learn the Way of the Buddha is to learn about oneself.
> To learn about oneself is to forget oneself.
> To forget oneself is to be enlightened by everything in the world.
> To be enlightened by everything in the world is to let go of one's body and mind.
> This essence is an unbroken stream of pure consciousness.

Thou standest alone! The obstinacy knoweth not that bliss, when the gods and thou and all thou hast, thy world, thy heavens, are enfolded in one embracing unity.

> In me is God, a fire
> And I in him its glow;
> In common is our life
> Apart we cannot grow.

> Meister Eckhardt

The enlightened person will become aware that everything is an expression of God, a virgin spirit from the absolute. Spirit of Spirit, begotten (caused to exist), not created.

Acknowledge God, Self, "Being," your true nature, and bring it to light. A person by nature is a giving person; and, when one withholds that which he has the power to give, because of fear of rejection or to gain control, he fosters a partition deep within himself that must be abolished.

> You often say, "I would give, but only to the deserving." The trees in your orchard say not so, nor the flocks in your pasture. They give that they may live, for to withhold is to perish.[13]

> Your earth is partitioned but in contrition, it is the partition in your hearts that you must abolish.

Once man turns his back on his true Self, his soul begins to disintegrate. He is no longer spiritually human; but, before this stage is reached, he may suffer for his stupidity, and the pain of suffering may lead him to realize the folly of his actions and return and claim his divine nature and bring this wisdom to light.

> Until this dog, the separate-self, can be subdued,
> Our life is folly, endlessly renewed.[1]

Man must take responsibility for his own actions in order to be free. God does not punish us. We punish ourselves. Those who are in hell are there by their own choice. Hell is the absence of God: to be loveless, to be abandoned, to have forfeited one's interdependence. To live only for oneself. No fire and brimstone can equal this desolation. God has no need to do anything to us. We are our own worst enemy. We are our own punisher. We create our own Hell. We either become what we were meant to be, or go to our death without ever having known what it was to live.

They could walk away from it if they would choose the difficult path of psychological independence but it is perhaps the most difficult and painful psychological task a human being can be called to face. Most fail and so remain its victims. They remain in hell because it seems safe and easy to them.

People of the Lie, M. Scott Peck

They would rather reign in hell than serve in heaven.

The hero king in his long nights of adventure in the graveyard carrying corpses of his past selves. He finally passes the macabre test and the veil of ignorance is lifted. During the following years, his earthy life was enlarged in virtue and glory.

The mystery of life is beyond all human conception. The higher the consciousness, the more the veil of mystery is lifted. In this consciousness, the reunion of the soul with God is the second birth. One must be born twice to find salvation, a sense of Self-realization.

> The secret waits for the insight
> Eyes unclouded by longing
> Those who cling to desires
> See only the outside container.

Our search for salvation lies in the renunciation of all desires conceived by the ego. It is the death of our separate-self. The only true salvation is for the mind to let go and lose itself.

> For whoever wants to save his life will lose it andwhoever loses his life for my sake will find it.
>
> Matthew 16:25

He who humbles himself shall be saved
He who bends shall be made straight
He who empties himself shall be filled

If we are successful and achieve this death of the ego (the mind, our illusory self), then our dread of death, the second death (the death of the mortal body) will have lost its terror of the unknown and the overwhelmingness of life. We will then bring to life and experience our second birth. It is a rebirth of the eternal spirit in all mankind by the touch of the Master's hand.

The Touch of the Master's Hand

'Twas battered and scarred, and the auctioneer
Thought it scarcely worth his while
To waste much time on the old violin,
But held it up with a smile:
"What am I bidden, good folks," he cried,
"Who'll start the bidding for me?"
"A dollar, A dollar", then, "Two!" "Only two?
Two dollars and who'll make it three?
Three dollars, once; three dollars, twice;
Going for three—" But no,
From the room, far back, a gray-haired man,
Came forward and picked up the bow;
Then, wiping the dust from the old violin,
And tightening the loose strings,
He played a melody pure and sweet
As a caroling angel sings.

The music ceased, and the auctioneer,
With a voice that was quiet and low,
Said: "What am I bid for the old violin?"
And he held it up with the bow.
"A thousand dollars, and who'll make it two?

Two thousand! And who'll make it three?
Three thousand, once, three thousand, twice,
And going, and gone," said he.
The people cheered, but some of them cried,
"We do not quite understand
What changed its worth?" Swift came the reply:
"The touch of the Master's hand."

And many a man with life out of tune,
And battered and scarred with sin,
Is auctioned cheap to the thoughtless crowd,
Much like the old violin.
A "mess of pottage," a glass of wine;
A game—and he travels on.
He is "going" once, "going" twice,
He's "going" and almost "gone."
But the master comes, and the foolish crowd
Never can quite understand
The worth of a soul and the change that's wrought
By the touch of the Master's hand.

Myra Brooks Welch

It is a touch which gives the soul dignity. A self-realized soul is one that has been touched by the hand of God and surrendered to a power within and beyond itself.

The miracle of our Being is to be what we really are meant to be. Our true spiritual nature is one of love and inner peace. Release this magnificent splendor, this love, this divine light, this celestial union that has always been there. Do not hide it under a bushel. Hiding love (this light under a bushel) is love unrecognized. Love is inexhaustible.

You are the light of the world. A city that is set on a hill cannot be hid.

Neither do men light a lamp and put it under a bushel, but on a stand, and it gives light to all that are in the house.

Let your light so shine before men, that they may see your good works, and give glory to your Father who is in heaven.

Matthew 5:14-16

The life of man has a divine origin. The only meaning of life is to be attained by living in the light that is within, and not putting it under a bushel, but by holding it high before people, so that they may see it.

One comes to realize that one never possesses a metaphysical belief, but is possessed by it. This awareness is analogous to a metamorphosis. There is a God potential in every man. Only through self-awareness will one come to recognize and claim Him. If one did not see the caterpillar become a butterfly, if one did not see the egg become a chicken, if one did not see the acorn grow into an oak tree, one would not believe that the chicken is the potential of the egg, the oak tree the potential of the acorn, and the butterfly the potential of the caterpillar. Then why is it so difficult to believe, and strange to understand, that God is the potential of man and man's true destiny is to become divine?

There he stands, A God in ruins!

"You have a low opinion of mankind, Stranger," and he answered: "Be not amazed, but forgive me: I was comparing them with the Gods."

Ye are gods.   John 10:34

What then is to become of man? Will he be equal with God or with the beasts?

I have of late,—but wherefore I know not,—lost all my mirth, foregone all custom of exercises; and, indeed it goes so heavily with my disposition that this goodly frame the earth, look you this, brave o'erhanging firmament, this majestical roof, fretted with golden fire,—why, it seems no other thing to me than a foul and pestilent congregation of vapors.

What a piece of work is man! How infinite in faculties! in form and moving, how express and admirable! in action, how like an angel! in movement, how like a God! the beauty of the world! the paragon of animals! And yet, to me, what is this quintessence of dust?[4]

We are born that we might become, as a conscious individual, a new life form of God. Die before you die is a breakthrough from the finite world of "Becoming" to the infinite world of "Being."

To die before you die is dying to your separate-self. The seed dies in order to experience itself as a tree or flower. The caterpillar dies in order to become a beautiful butterfly. The acorn dies in order to become an oak tree. The egg dies in order for it to become a chicken. Man must also die to his separate-self (ego) in order to experience his true Self in God. In essence the seed did not die, it evolved. Man does not die, he unfolds, free from all limitation.

The finite temporal transient self forgets its limited life in the boundless ocean of eternal consciousness and evolves to his (His) perfection. It is not a death but a victory over death. It is an arising and a resurrection.

The resurrection is the elevated and awakened state of consciousness from the primitive, social, individual, and cosmic-universal state of mind to the transcendental truth of His "Being." It is a life entirely in and of the Spirit. For those who experience God become God conscious. A direct experience beyond the level of the mind. One no longer contemplates reality, one becomes reality. To know God instead of worshiping him, to be the world instead of encountering it and accept death now instead of fearing it tomorrow. If you are your experience, you are the world so experienced.

Knowing the One, one knows all.

Only the pure in heart shall see God. Only through Self awareness of a higher form of consciousness will one come to recognize and claim Him.

> That which we seek with passionate longing, here and there, upwards and downwards, we find at last within ourselves. The kingdom of heaven, the kingdom within! The indwelling God!

If it is true that we are made in the likeness and image of God, then what is the law of the "Divine Nature" must be the law of ours also, and, as we awake to this, we become partakers of the "Divine Nature."

> The great God dreamed a dream through me, mighty as a dream of God could be. He made me a victorious man, shaped me into a perfect plan, summoned me forth to radiant birth upon this earth. He lavished gifts within my hand, gave me power to command the thundering forces that he hurled upon this seething world. Creation's dream was wondrous good, had I but understood. The great God dreamed a dream through me, but I was blind and could not see. My royal gifts were laid to rust, for parentage, I claimed the dust, decay and sorrow, age and blight, these gifts I dreamed my right. The great God spoke a word through me, that word was life, how can it be that I, in God's own substance made, should face the universe afraid? Born of eternal life am I, why should I fail and die? Oh, God, so huge was thy intent, so

great was the passing spent. This counterfeit is not
the plan, that thou didst dream for man. 'Tis this,
man's dream, must mate with thine. Man's word,
man's life must be divine. Man must be conscious
through and through to make thy dream come true.

Angela Morgan

Looking for the maker of this tabernacle
I ran to no avail
Through a round of many births;
And wearisome is birth again and again.
But now, maker of the tabernacle, thou hast been seen;
Thou shalt not rear this tabernacle again.
All thy rafters are broken,
The ridge-pole is shattered;
The mind approaching the Eternal.
Attained to the extinction of all desires.

———————

    Many a house of life
Hath held me—seeking ever him who wrought
These prisons of the senses, sorrow—fraught;
    Sore was my ceaseless strife!
    But now,
Thou builder of the tabernacle—thou!
    I know thee! Never shalt thou build again
    These walls of pain,
Nor raise the roof-tree of deceits, nor lay
    Fresh rafters on the clay;
Broken thy house is and the ridge-pole split!
    Delusion fashioned it!
    Safe pass I thence—deliverance to obtain.

Buddha

Deliverance and salvation are a communion of Truth—one of experiencing the center of the conscious universe. Herein lies man's true destiny, freedom, and immortality. We are part of the whole, and the whole is God. The part has meaning only within the whole, and we as humans already exist within the whole of "Being."

> As flesh remains an agent of the soul,
> Your soul's an agent of the sacred whole.[1]

Man will then experience himself as the whole, completely submitted to the will and the laws of the whole.

> How can we know the infinite? God? Being? Not by reason. You can only apprehend the infinite by a power greater than reason. By entering into a state in which you are your finite self no longer. In which the divine essence is communicated to you. This is Ecstasy. It is the liberation of your mind from the finite consciousness. When you thus cease to be finite, you become one with the infinite. In the reduction of your soul to its simplest self, its divine essence, you realize this.
>
> Plotinus

> You cannot take hold of it, nor can you get rid of it; while you can do neither, it goes its own way.
>
> Yung-chia Ta-shin

The mind can only analyze, the heart synthesizes. The mind divides. Only the heart gives unity. A true man follows the path of love and lives in the present. The mind lives in the past and future. One has to go beyond the mind to experience God.

Lose yourself in the stream of life, in the natural order of the universe, experiencing and expressing the one unity. Be and live spontaneously in the present moment. Therefore, the only goal in life is living.

When we have broken with the god of tradition and ceased from our god of rhetoric and cease worshiping god with our intellect. That which Is really God fires us with His presence.

Ralph Waldo Emerson

Listen to the exhortation of the dawn. Look to this day. For it is life, the very life of life. In its brief course lie all the verities and realities of your existence. The bliss of growth. The glory of action. The splendor of beauty. For yesterday is but a dream and tomorrow is only a vision. But today well lived makes every yesterday a dream of happiness. And every tomorrow a vision of hope. Look well therefore to this day! Such is the salutation of the dawn.

Man is truly God, and God is man. Whoever does not hold God as an inner possession and only sees him outside of himself does not have Him at all. This man becomes troubled, and this trouble lies within himself. He has not as yet experienced and claimed the existence of God within. If he had, then he would feel at ease in all places, and secure with all people.

All gleams and flashes of a superior Self-awareness are higher states of consciousness (the heights of harmony and beauty), and give an unheard of, and until then, undreamed of feeling of wholeness, harmony and beauty. It is an ecstatic and prayer-like union in the highest synthesis of life. This realization within ourselves is the higher aim of mankind.

The highest attainment of life is not action. It is not a question of doing. It is simply a question of "Being," in which time has ceased, and in which the instant expands itself indefinitely, as in the inspired state of the artist.

To see the world in a grain of sand,
And a heaven in a wild flower;
Hold infinity in the palm of your hand,
And eternity in an hour.

William Blake

Artists, poets, and scientists have a high degree of sensitivity because of which they are able to see more than meets the eye of the common observer. For them God is as real as any dream that has come true.

The heart is the temple where all truth arises. A truth has been revealed to me that defies an adequate description. Love is a privilege that makes everything beautiful, noble, and pure. When you love, everything reminds you of the one you love. Love is of God and knoweth God.

Philosophers have dreamed, mystics have seen, prophets have transmitted.

> Two sages were standing on a bridge over a stream. One said to the other, "I wish I were a fish, they are so happy!" The second sage replied, "How do you know whether fish are happy of not? You are not a fish." The first sage said, "But you are not me, so how do you know whether I know how fish feel?"

One that is attempting to understand and relate to the experience of God is like the second sage who might reply, "How do you know that God exists, you have never experienced His love and presence?" The first sage would reply, "But you are not me, so how do you know whether I have had the experience or not?"

Denial of the reality of the experience, or criticism of certain of its aspects, is inadmissible from a man who has no direct knowledge of the experience.

You are asking me if there are any answers. I hear you and I answer that I cannot answer. The answers are blowing in the wind. You must find the answer yourself. The deepest question remains unanswered. It is like unto:

> A Spirit that blows across the water, stirring up
> the waves as a heart is stirred by the thoughts
> of love.
>
> George Rapanos

Those who experience God are elevated to a higher state of consciousness and are unable to express its actual significance. They realize the impossibility of describing the experience. God was present, though invisible; He fell under none of my senses, yet my consciousness perceived Him and all that exists.

> I saw and heard and knew at last
> The How and Why of all things, past,
> And present, and forevermore.
> The Universe; cleft to the core,
> Lay open to my probing sense.[3]

> O happy living things! no tongue
> Their beauty might declare:
> A spring of love gushed from my heart,
> And I blessed them unaware:
> Sure my kind saint took pity on me,
> And I blessed them unaware.[2]

The experience of a union with the higher power gives you a testament to the truth which reflects the immortality of the eternal spirit of God. This is recognized by the fruit it bears.

> Life is short, and this earthly existence has but
> a single fruit to yield—holiness within, and
> selfless action without.
>
> Meditations Marcus Aurelius

You are now aware that you are a reflection of God, as well as a biological entity, and must grow as a child in this spiritual awareness, as you grew as a child in social consciousness.

There is no cure for man in his present social and psychological condition. He is a victim. He is trapped in a world that is a breeding ground for hyperdistended egos. His only hope is the possession of a higher state of consciousness, the awareness of a spirit greater than the forces that now move him—not the force of action but a condition of "Being." God is everywhere present in spirit and in truth, within and without.

> It moves, It moves not.
> It is far, and It is near.
> It is within all this,
> And It is outside of all this.

Isa-Upanishad

The supreme consciousness of God as "Being" lives in the world diffused among all the living souls on earth, striving ever to lead them to a recognition of the real Self, the Spirit within. He is with us as an abiding spirit, a comforter, a helper, an elder brother. He is here with us now and forever in actual spiritual communion.

The spirit of God, Christ, Buddha, Mohammed, Krishna, Chuang-tse, Lao-tse, as well as that of all creation, comes of a virgin spirit, from an unutterable source of existence.

A virgin birth is dying to our separate-self. This virgin Spirit is incarnated in our bodies and there begins the life of man, not fully aware of his own nature, but gradually awakening into knowledge and consciousness, just as does every human soul, until at last the true nature of His "Being" bursts upon Him and sees that he is indeed God incarnate.

> Truly, Thou art a God who hides himself.

Isaiah 45:15

Each man has within himself the capacity to awake and be enlightened. It is the basic nature of human beings, but lies asleep in the depths of the soul. God descended into man so that man may become divine, and, through man's own self-awareness, will he acknowledge and receive this gift of love.

The God within you is like the fabled Hindu God who descends into the body of a pig and then forgets himself. It is to bring you to the realization that you are a God and not a pig. His spirit is working within your soul. Have you never heard his voice, crying from within your soul, "Come out, come out of your pig nature and realize the God that you really are!"

He does but sleep. Wake Him!

The God in each person is ever-present, but unrealized and lies, as it were, asleep in the depths of the soul. It is the presence and awareness of the divine force within you that constitutes salvation and redemption. Salvation and redemption for all mankind has to be personally earned and granted by the Grace of God to each individual.

> It takes
> So many thousand years to wake,
> But will you wake for pity's sake...?[6]

A Sleep of Prisoners

Like an acorn from the parent oak, we have fallen to the earth. It is here that our latent potentialities are germinated by the physical elements. Through the intelligence and power inherent in our nature, our latent possibilities unfold; and, in time, we develop into a majestic splendor of the mighty parent from which we are created. The potential of the oak tree lies vibrating in the atomic structure of the acorn. Within you lies the seed that may mature into God.

> You are a temple of God and the spirit of God dwelleth in you.

God's presence and guidance dwell with mankind. Divine guidance is available to those who seek it from their hearts, humbly and devoutly.

> Ask, and it will be given you;
> Seek, and you will find;
> Knock, and it will be opened to you.

Matthew 7:7

The kingdom of God is within you. Prayer and meditation in silence are the means by which one enters the cosmic-universal mind. By asking, you create the bridge between you and God. For God is at the center of all life! An all-embracing unity.

> For every one who asks receives,
> And he who seeks finds,
> And to him who knocks it will be opened.

Matthew 7:8

All we have to do is reaffirm the existence of the absolute within us and claim Him as our divine right. Just as we awaken into a perception of Divine Nature, so shall the human race awaken in time, returning to the root and the source of His existence. As a child grows in self-consciousness, so will man grow, like the child, in spiritual consciousness, until he elevates himself to a state of spiritual, trans-personal, ultimate, and absolute consciousness.

You are a child of the universe, no less than the trees and the stars; you have a right to be here. And whether or not it is clear to you, no doubt the universe is unfolding as it should. Therefore, be at peace with God, whatever you conceive Him to be. Whatever your labors and aspirations, in the noisy confusion of life keep peace with your soul.

Desiderata

The highest form of man is not the ascetic who remains in almost perpetual isolation and contemplation, but rather a man who lives in the world out of compassion and social justice for others, working to share with them his vision and his own state of consciousness.

Let there be peace on earth and let it begin with me.

From Him we come, with Him we are included, to Him we go, in Him we shall find all heaven and lasting joy. We should be wise enough to perceive Him, gentle enough to receive Him, and faithful enough to keep ourselves in Him, and have faith that His will is with us always.

The more clearly the soul sees the blessed face by grace and love, the more it longs to see it in its fullness. The faithful can have visions only in the form of faith they profess. The Christian will see it differently from the Muslim, Hindu, or Jew.

This earth is partitioned, but in contrition it is the partitions in our hearts that we must abolish if we are to experience God as our eternal "Being." There is no issue stronger than the tissue of love, and no need as holy as the palm outstretched in the run of generosity.

> I am not in heaven, I am here, hear me; I am in you, feel me; I am with you, see me; I am for you, need me. I am all mankind and only through kindness will you reach me.

A true spiritual person worships God in any form of religion for the Truth is the same, no matter under what name it is taught, or who teaches it. The Path is not in the rosary, the prayer-mat or the robe.

If god is the god of love, it seems most likely he would have revealed himself to all his children.

Go home to your knees, and worship me in any cloth,
for I was never tailor-made. Who told you I was?
Who gave you the right to believe it?

Truth is one; the sages speak of it by many names.

Strip it of the personal colorings of the teacher, and it seems to be the same. One of truth, and the love of God for all mankind.

The integration of the Spirit and soul (its wholeness) becomes the supreme goal upon which the fate of humanity depends. Unless God and His love are the first and the last, mankind will never be left in peace.

For love is of God, and everyone that loveth is born of God and knoweth God. For love is the messenger between God and man. It is love alone that unites the soul with God; and nothing is of the nature of true virtue, in which love and ultimate consciousness is not the first and last.

The door is always open for those who choose to seek Him.

unto whom all hearts are open,
unto whom all wills do speak,
from whom no secret thing is hidden,
I beseech thee
so to cleanse the purpose of my heart
with the unutterable gift of thy grace
that I may perfectly love thee,
and worthily praise thee.

God is One,
Living, eternal, and besides Him none.

The Lord's Prayer

Our Father,	Man is the son of the Father.
Which art in heaven,	God is the infinite spiritual source of life.
Hallowed be Thy name,	May the Source of Life be held holy.
Thy kingdom come,	May His power be established over all men.
Thy will be done, as in heaven,	May His will be fulfilled, as it is in Himself,
So also on earth.	So also in the bodily life.
Give us our daily bread	The temporal life is the food of the true life.
This day.	The true life is in the present.
And forgive us our debts as we forgive our debtors,	May the faults and errors of the past not hide this true life from us,
And lead us not into temptation,	And may they not lead us into delusion,
But deliver us from evil,	So that no evil may come to us,
For Thine is the kingdom, the power, and the glory.	And there shall be order, and strength, and reason.

The Gospel in Brief
Leo Tolstoi

The son God. Man, the son of God, is powerless in the flesh, and free in the spirit.

Life in the Spirit. Man must work, not for the flesh, but for the spirit.

The Source of Life. The life of all men has proceeded from the spirit of the Father.

God's Kingdom. Therefore the will of the Father is the life and welfare of all men.

The true life. The fulfilment of the personal will leads to death; the fulfilment of the Father's will gives the true life.

The false life. Therefore, in order to receive the true life, man must on earth resign the false life of the flesh, and live by the Spirit.

I and the Father are one. The true food of everlasting life is the fulfillment of the Father's will.

Life is not temporal. Therefore true life is to be lived in the present.

Temptations. The illusions of temporal life conceal from men the true life in the present.

The warfare with temptation. Therefore, not to fall by temptation, we must, at every moment of life, be at one with the Father.

The farewell discourse. The self-life is an illusion which comes through the flesh, an evil. The true life is the life common to all men.

The victory of the spirit over the flesh. Therefore for him who lives, not the self-life, but a common life in the will of the Father, there is no death. Bodily death is for him union with the Father.

The Gospel in Brief
Leo Tolstoi

Seven Impurities of the Soul

Pride—is the greatest of all sins because pride misguides you by arrogance, haughtiness and an over evaluation of one's self and contempt for others. Pride prevents you from realizing the need for the journey and that there exists something greater than your separate-self.

Sloth—is laziness. Sloth is the crime of omission. Sloth is what prevents you from beginning the journey that will lead to the Self-purification of the soul.

Hate—is a strong feeling of dislike or ill will.

Greed—is an excess desire, especially for wealth.

Envy and Jealousy—are feelings of discontent and resentment aroused by another's desirable possessions or qualities, accompanied by a strong desire to have them for oneself. Jealousy is resentful and suspicious of rivalry.

Gluttony—is an excess beyond one's need.

Lust—is to feel an intense desire.

Seven Valleys of the Quest

"The Conference of the Birds" is the best-known work of the Persian poet Farid ud-Din Attar. It is a lengthy poem about a quest for an ideal spiritual king and an affirmation that only God truly exists. All other things are an emanation of Him, or are His "shadow."

Religion is useful mainly as a way of reaching to a Truth beyond the teachings of particular religions. Man's distinctions between good and evil have no meaning for God, who knows only Unity. The soul is trapped within the cage of the body, but can, by looking inward, become aware of its essential nature and find freedom in its affinity with God.

The awakened soul, guided by God's grace, can progress along a "Way" which leads to annihilation in God. The story is about individual effort as well as grace and the fact that both are necessary for spiritual progress.

Two themes in particular are diffused throughout most of the poem. The necessity for destroying the self, and the importance of passionate love. The self is seen as an entity dependent on pride and reputation. There can be no progress until the pilgrim is indifferent to both, and the commonest way of making him indifferent is the experience of overwhelming love.

One must traverse seven valleys before he is able to journey into the heart of God. He must discipline himself to achieve purification from his passions and desires to compassion and love.

> The first stage is the valley of the Quest;
> Then Love's wide valley is our second test;
> The third is Insight into Mystery,
> The fourth Detachment and Serenity—
> The fifth is Unity; the sixth is Awe,
> A deep Bewilderment unknown before,

The seventh Poverty and Nothingness—
And there you are suspended, motionless,
Till you are drawn—the impulse is not yours—
A drop absorbed in seas that have no shores.

The Valley of the Quest

When you begin the valley of the quest
Misfortunes will deprive you of all rest.

The Valley of Love

Love's valley is the next, and here desire
Will plunge the pilgrim into seas of fire.

The Valley of Insight into Mystery

The next broad valley which the traveller sees
Brings insight into the mysteries;
Here every pilgrim takes a different way,
And different spirits different rules obey.

There are so many roads, and each is fit
For that one pilgrim who must follow it.
How could a spider or a tiny ant
Tread the same path as some huge elephant?

Our pathways differ—no bird ever knows
The secret route by which another goes.
Our insight comes to us by different signs,
One prays in mosques and one in idols' shrines—
But when Truth's sunlight clears the upper air,
Each pilgrim sees that he is welcomed there.
His essence will shine forth; the world that seemed
A furnace will be sweeter than he dreamed.

The heart of all he sees, there will ascend
The longed-for face of the immortal Friend.
A hundred thousand secrets will be known
When that unveiled, surpassing face is shown—
A hundred thousand men must faint and fail
Till one shall draw aside the secrets' veil—
Perfected, of rare courage he must be
To dive through that immense, uncharted sea.
If you discern such hidden truths and feel
Joy flood your life, do not relax your zeal;
Though thirst is quenched, though you are bathed in bliss
Beyond all possible hypothesis,
Though you should reach the throne of God, implore
Him still unceasingly: "Is there yet more?"
Now let the sea of gnosis drown your mind,
Or dust and death are all that you will find.
If you ignore our quest and idly sleep,
You will not glimpse the Friend; rise now and weep.
And if you cannot find His beauty here,
Seek out Truth's mysteries and persevere!

The Valley of Detachment

Next comes the Valley of Detachment; here
All claims, all lust for meaning disappear.

Renounce the work you know, the tasks you've done,
And learn which tasks to work at, which to shun.
What words can guide you where you ought to turn?
It may be you will have the wit to learn;
But whether you lament or idly sing,
Act with detachment now in everything.
Detachment is a flame, a livid flash,
That will reduce a hundred worlds to ash;
Its valley makes creation disappear,
And if the world has gone, then where is fear?

The Valley of Unity

Next comes the Valley of pure Unity,
A place of lonely, long austerity,
And all who enter on this waste have found
Their various necks by one tight collar bound—
If you see many here or but a few,
They're one, however they appear to you.
The many here are merged in one; one form
Involves the multifarious, thick swarm
(This is the oneness of diversity,
No oneness locked in singularity);
Unit and number here have passed away;
Forget for-ever and Creation's day—
That day is gone; eternity is gone;
Let them depart into oblivion.

When once the pilgrim has attained this stage,
He will have passed beyond mere pilgrimage;
He will be lost and dumb—for God will speak,
The God whom all these wandering pilgrims seek—
Beyond all notions of the part, the Whole,
Of qualities and the essential soul.

To glimpse this secret is to turn aside
From both worlds, from all egocentric pride.

The Valley of Bewilderment

Next comes the Valley of Bewilderment,
A place of pain and gnawing discontent—
Each second you will sigh, and every breath
Will be a sword to make you long for death;
Blinded by grief, you will not recognize
The days and nights that pass before your eyes.

The Unity you knew has gone; your soul
Is scattered and knows nothing of the Whole.
If someone asks: "What is our present state;
Is drunkenness or sober sense your fate,
And do you flourish now or fade away?"
The pilgrim will confess: "I cannot say;
I have no certain knowledge any more;
I doubt my doubt, doubt itself is unsure;
I love, but who is it for whom I sigh?
Not Moslem, yet not heathen; who am I?
My heart is empty, yet with love is full;
My own love is to me incredible."

My heart is lost, and here I cannot find
That rope by which men live, the rational mind—
The key to thought is lost; to reach this far
Means to despair of who and what you are.
And yet it is to see within the soul—
And at a stroke—the meaning of the Whole."

To those who ask: "What can I do?" reply:
"Bid all that you have done till now goodbye!"
Once in the Valley of Bewilderment
The pilgrim suffers endless discontent,
Crying: "How long must I endure delay,
Uncertainty? When shall I see the Way?
When shall I know? O, when?" But knowledge here
Is turned again to indecisive fear.

The Valley of Poverty and Nothingness

Next comes that valley words cannot express,
The Vale of Poverty and Nothingness:
Here you are lame and deaf, the mind has gone;
You enter an obscure oblivion.
When sunlight penetrates the atmosphere
A hundred thousand shadows disappear,

Whoever sinks within this sea is blest
And in self-loss obtains eternal rest;
The heart that would be lost in this wide sea
Disperses in profound tranquility,
And if it should emerge again it knows
The secret ways in which the world arose.
The pilgrim who has grown wise in the Quest,
The sufi who has weathered every test.

He is not, yet he is; what could this mean?
It is a state the mind has never seen.

> Excerpts from "The Conference of the Birds."
> Farid un-Din Attar

Stages Mystics Undergo

1

Sudden conversion, "the awakening of the Self," a sudden realization of a strikingly new and different emotional experience that seems to exist beyond sensation and that carries with it the awareness of a "higher" more desirable level of experience. It is "a breakthrough" of the transmarginal consciousness, the sudden "possession of an active subliminal self" (below the threshold of conscious perception).

2

After the mystic experiences this deep level of consciousness, he finds that his former patterns of living are no longer satisfying. He feels that his old connections to the social reality must be purged or mortified. "The Purification of the Self." The new subliminal consciousness with which the person has just come into contact is markedly different from the everyday consciousness of his ordinary experience. The goal of mortification for the mystic is life, but this life can only come through the "death" of the "old self."

3

"The Illumination of the Self." Here he experiences more fully what lies beyond the boundaries of his immediate senses. A joyous apprehension of what the mystic experiences to be the Absolute, including effulgent outpouring of ecstasy and rapture in which the individual glories in his relationship with the Absolute. What distinguishes this stage from later stages, however, is that the person still experiences himself as a separate entity, not yet unified with what he considers to be the Ultimate. There is yet a sense of I-hood, of ego, of self.

4

The Dark Night of the Soul, "total negation and rejection of the joy of the preceding stage." The person feels very much alone and depressed. During this first purgative period the individual had to purge himself of his former attachments to the social world. Now he must purge himself of his experience of self. His very will must become totally submerged to the unknown "force" he experiences within. As long as he asserts his own will or individuality, he is maintaining distance or separateness from what he feels to be the Ultimate.

5

The complete and total absorption in the asocial, personal world, what has been called "the Unitive Life." It consists of the obliteration of the senses and even the sense of self, resulting in the experience of unity with the universe. This state has been described as a state of pure consciousness, in which the individual experiences nothing (no-thing). The individual has seemingly made contact with the deepest regions of his consciousness and experiences the process as having been completed. Emotionally the person feels totally tranquil and at peace.

6

The return of the mystic from the experience of oneness with the universe to the requirements of social living constitutes the most important part of his path. In most mystics, it may be observed that they renew their practical involvement in social situations with a new vitality and strength. Example; "Martha and Mary must work together when they offer the Lord lodging" implies that material and spiritual involvement are equally important. Buddha returned from his ecstasy underneath the Bo tree to the social world from which he had fled. The mystic now no longer finds his involvement with the world to be abhorrent, but in fact, seems to welcome the opportunity to move in that social world he has abandoned.

To argue with someone that he should follow the way of the mystics is as silly as to argue with an unripe apple that it is time that it should fall from the tree. When the apple is ready, it will not need to be told that it should fall; it will do so quite on its own accord.

Tablets with the Ten Commandments
recall God's covenant with Israel

FOUR NOBLE TRUTHS
The fundamental teachings of Gautama the Buddha.

He who recognizes the existence of suffering.
He who recognizes its cause.
He who recognizes its remedy.
He that recognizes its cessation has fathomed the four noble truths.

NOBLE EIGHTFOLD PATH
The destruction of suffering

Right views.
Right aspirations.
Right speech.
Right behavior.
Right livelihood.
Right effort.
Right thoughts.
Right contemplation.

Buddha

Said the Lord, "I am Alpha and Omega,
the beginning and the ending . . ."

"I will be with you always"

PSALM 23

The Lord is my shepherd; I shall not want.

He maketh me to lie down in green pastures: he leadeth me beside the still waters.

He restoreth my soul: he leadeth me in the paths of righteousness for his name's sake.

Yea, though I walk through the valley of the shadow of death, I will fear not evil: for thou art with me; thy rod and thy staff they comfort me.

Thou preparest a table before me in the presence of mine enemies: thou anointest my head with oil; my cup runneth over.

Surely goodness and mercy shall follow me all the days of my life: and I will dwell in the house of the Lord forever.

May your feet tread the roads
   Of a long delight;
May your eyes see beauty,
May your soul see light.
May your lips know a smile,
   And your heart know a song;
   And love go with you
   Your whole life long.

NOTES

1   Farid-un-Attar, The Conference of the Birds.

2   Samuel Taylor Coleridge, The Rime of the Ancient Mariner.

3   Edna St. Vincent Millay, Renascence.

4   William Shakespeare

5   Richard Jefferies

6   Christopher Fry, A Sleep of Prisoners.

7   Zohar

8   Karlfied Graf Durckheim

9   George Rapanos

10   Charles C. Converse

11   W. W. Walford

12   H. F. Lyte

13   Ella Wheeler Wilcox, Ad Finem

14   Algernon Charles Swinburne

15   Ibid 18:4